FROM INTELLECT TO INTUITION

BOOKS BY ALICE A. BAILEY

Initiation, Human and Solar
Letters on Occult Meditation
The Consciousness of the Atom
A Treatise on Cosmic Fire
The Light of the Soul
The Soul and Its Mechanism
From Intellect to Intuition
A Treatise on White Magic
From Bethlehem to Calvary
Discipleship in the New Age — Vol. I
Discipleship in the New Age — Vol. II
Problems of Humanity
The Reappearance of the Christ
The Destiny of the Nations
Glamour: A World Problem
Telepathy and the Etheric Vehicle
The Unfinished Autobiography
Education in the New Age
The Externalisation of the Hierarchy
A Treatise on the Seven Rays:
Vol. I — Esoteric Psychology
Vol. II — Esoteric Psychology
Vol. III — Esoteric Astrology
Vol. IV — Esoteric Healing
Vol. V—The Rays and the Initiations

FROM INTELLECT
TO INTUITION

ALICE A. BAILEY

LUCIS PUBLISHING COMPANY
New York

LUCIS PRESS, LTD.
London

First Printing, 1932
Ninth Printing, 1972 (First Paperback Edition)
Fourteenth Printing, 1997

ISBN No. 0-85330-108-5
Library of Congress Catalog Card Number: 32-16728

The publication of this book is financed by the Tibetan Book Fund which is established for the perpetuation of the teachings of the Tibetan and Alice A. Bailey.

This Fund is controlled by the Lucis Trust, a tax-exempt, religious, educational corporation.

The Lucis Publishing Company is a non-profit organisation owned by the Lucis Trust. No royalties are paid on this book.

This title is also available in a
clothbound edition.

It has been translated into Croatian, Danish, Dutch, Finnish, French, German, Greek, Italian, Polish, Portuguese, Romanian, Russian, and Spanish. Translation into other languages is proceeding.

LUCIS PUBLISHING COMPANY
120 Wall Street
New York, NY 10005

LUCIS PRESS, LTD.
Suite 54
3 Whitehall Court
London SWlA 2EF

MANUFACTURED IN THE UNITED STATES OF AMERICA
By FORT ORANGE PRESS, INC., Albany, NY

TABLE OF CONTENTS

THE GREAT INVOCATION

From the point of Light within the Mind of God
Let light stream forth into the minds of men.
Let Light descend on Earth.

From the point of Love within the Heart of God
Let love stream forth into the hearts of men.
May Christ return to Earth.

From the centre where the Will of God is known
Let purpose guide the little wills of men —
The purpose which the Masters know and serve.

From the centre which we call the race of men
Let the Plan of Love and Light work out
And may it seal the door where evil dwells.

Let Light and Love and Power restore the Plan on Earth.

"The above Invocation or Prayer does not belong to any person or group but to all Humanity. The beauty and the strength of this Invocation lies in its simplicity, and in its expression of certain central truths which all men, innately and normally, accept — the truth of the existence of a basic Intelligence to Whom we vaguely give the name of God; the truth that behind all outer seeming, the motivating power of the universe is Love; the truth that a great Individuality came to earth, called by Christians, the Christ, and embodied that love so that we could understand; the truth that both love and intelligence are effects of what is called the Will of God; and finally the self-evident truth that only through *humanity* itself can the Divine Plan work out."

ALICE A. BAILEY

CHAPTER ONE

INTRODUCTORY THOUGHTS

"The scientific method—apart from a narrowly agnostic and pragmatist point of view—is therefore by itself incomplete and insufficient: it demands in order to make contact with reality the complement of some metaphysic or other."

JOSEPH MARÉCHAL, S.J.

Introductory Thoughts

The present widespread interest in the subject of Meditation is an evidence of a world need which requires clear understanding. Where we find a popular trend in any particular direction, which is one-pointed and steady, it may be safe to assume that out of it will emerge that which the race needs in its onward march. That meditation is regarded, by those who define loosely, as a "mode of prayer" is, unfortunately, true. But it can be demonstrated that in the right understanding of the meditation process and in its right adaptation to the needs of our modern civilization will be found the solution of the present educational impasse and the method whereby the fact of the soul may be ascertained—that living something which we call the "Soul" for lack of a better term.

The purpose of this book is to deal with the nature and true significance of meditation, and with its use on a large scale in the West. It is suggested that it may eventually supplant the present methods of memory training, and prove a potent factor in modern educational procedure. It is a subject that has engrossed the attention of thinkers in the East and in the West for thousands of years, and this uniformity of interest is in itself of importance. The next developments which will carry the race forward along the path of its unfolding consciousness must surely lie in the direction of synthesis. The growth of human knowledge must be brought about by the fusion of the Eastern and the Western techniques of mental training. This has already proceeded apace and thinkers in both hemispheres are realizing that this fusion is leading towards some most significant realization. Edward Carpenter says that:

"We seem to be arriving at a time when, with the circling of our knowledge of the globe, a great synthesis of all human thought . . . is quite naturally and inevitably taking place. . . . Out of this meeting of elements is already arising the dim outline of a philosophy which must surely dominate human thought for a long period."[1]

Herein lies the glory and hope of the race and the outstanding triumph of science. We are now one people. The heritage of any race lies open to another; the best thought of the centuries is available for all; and ancient techniques and modern methods must meet and interchange. Each will have to modify its mode of presentation and each will have to make an effort to understand the underlying spirit which has produced a peculiar phraseology and imagery, but when these concessions are made, a structure of truth will be found to emerge which will embody the spirit of the New Age. Modern thinkers are realizing this and Dr. Overstreet points out that:

[1] Carpenter, Edward, *The Art of Creation*, p. 7.

"Eastern philosophy, one suspects, has had small effect upon western thought chiefly because of its manner. But there is every reason to believe that as the influence of western thinking—particularly its experimental hard-headedness—is felt in the East, a new philosophic manner will be adopted, and the profound spirituality of eastern thought will be expressed in ways more acceptable to the western mind."[2]

Both schools have hitherto tended to antagonize each other, yet the quest for truth has been one; the interest in that which is, and that which can be, is not confined to either group; and the factors with which each has had to work have been the same. Though the mind of the eastern thinker may run to creative imagery and that of the western worker to creative scientific achievement, yet the world into which they enter is curiously the same; the instrument of thought which they employ is called the "mind" in the West and "mind-stuff" (chitta) in the East; both use the language of symbology to express their conclusions and both reach the point where words prove futile to embody the intuited possibilities.

Dr. Jung, one of the people who is seeking to bring these hitherto discordant elements together, touches on this in the following extract from his Commentary on an ancient Chinese writing. He says

"Western consciousness is by no means consciousness in general, but rather a historically conditioned, and geographically limited, factor, representative of only one part of humanity. The widening of our own consciousness ought

[2] Overstreet, H. A., *The Enduring Quest*, p. 271.

not to proceed at the expense of other kinds of consciousness, but ought to take place through the development of
those elements of our psyche which are analogous to those
of a foreign psyche, just as the East cannot do without our
technique, science and industry. The European invasion of
the East was a deed of violence on a great scale, and it has
left us the duty—*noblesse oblige*—of understanding the
mind of the East. This is perhaps more necessary than we
realize at present.''[3]

Dr. Hocking of Harvard also brings us the same
idea when he says:

''There seems reason to hope for a better physical future
of the race by the aid of a sound mental hygiene. After the
era of the charlatans has gone by, and to some extent by
their aid, there appears a possibility of steadily enlarging
self-mastery, as the spiritual sense of such discipline as the
Yoga joins with the sober elements of Western psychology
and a sane system of ethics. No one of these is worth much
without the others.''[4]

Those who have studied in both schools tell us
that the mystical imagery of the East (and also of
our Western mystical exponents) is only a veil behind which those gifted with intuitive perception
have always been able to penetrate. The science of
the West, with its emphasis upon the nature of the
form, has also led us into the realm of the intuition
and it would seem as if the two ways could blend and
that it should be possible for each—discarding the
non-essentials—to arrive at a basis of understand-

[3] Wilhelm, Richard, and Jung, Dr. C. G., *The Secret of the Golden
Flower*, p. 136.
[4] Hocking, Wm. E., *Self, Its Body and Freedom*, p. 75.

ing. Thus they work out a new approach to the central mystery of man founded on old and demonstrated truths. Dr. Jung again takes this up as follows:

"Science is the best tool of the Western mind and with it more doors can be opened than with bare hands. Thus it is part and parcel of our understanding and only clouds our insight when it lays claim to being the one and only way of comprehending. But it is the East that has taught us another, wider, more profound, and a higher understanding, that is, understanding through life. We know this way only vaguely, as a mere shadowy sentiment culled from religious terminology, and therefore we gladly dispose of Eastern 'wisdom' in quotation marks, and push it away into the obscure territory of faith and superstition. But in this way Eastern 'realism' is completely misunderstood. It does not consist of sentimental, exaggeratedly mystical, intuitions bordering on the pathological and emanating from ascetic recluses and cranks; the wisdom of the East is based on practical knowledge . . . which we have not the slightest justification for undervaluing."[5]

It is in the training of the mind that the crux of the situation lies. The human mind is apparently an instrument which we are able to use in two directions. One direction is outward. The mind, in this mode of functioning, registers our contacts with the physical and mental worlds in which we live, and recognizes emotional and sensory conditions. It is the recorder and correlator of our sensations, of our reactions, and of all that is conveyed to it via the five senses and the brain. This is a field of knowl-

[5] Wilhelm, Richard, and Jung, Dr. C. G., *The Secret of the Golden Flower*, p. 78.

edge that has been extensively studied, and much headway has been made by psychologists in understanding the processes of mentation. "Thinking," Dr. Jung tells us, "is one of the four basic psychological functions. It is that psychological function which, in accordance with its own laws, brings given presentations into conceptual connection. It is an apperceptive activity—both active and passive. Active thinking is an act of the will; passive thinking is an occurrence."[6]

As we shall see later, it is the thought apparatus which is involved in Meditation and which must be trained to add to this first function of the mind an ability to turn in another direction, and to register with equal facility the inner or intangible world. This ability to re-orient itself will enable the mind to register the world of subjective realities, of intuitive perception and of abstract ideas. This is the high heritage of the mystic, but seems as yet not to be within the grasp of the average man.

The problem facing the human family today in the realms both of science and of religion results from the fact that the follower of both schools finds he is standing at the portal of a metaphysical world. A cycle of development has come to an end. Man, as a thinking, feeling entity, seems now to have arrived at a fair measure of understanding the instrument with which he has to work. He is asking himself: What use is he to make of it? Where is the mind,

* Dibblee, George Binney, *Instinct and Intuition*, p. 85.

which he is slowly learning to master, going to lead him?

What does the future hold for man? Something, we feel, of greater beauty and certainty than anything we have hitherto known. Perhaps it will be a universal arrival at that knowledge which the individual mystic has had. Our ears are deafened by the din of our modern civilization and yet at times we catch those overtones which testify to a world which is immaterial. Our eyes are blinded by the fog and the smoke of our immediate foreground, yet there do come flashes of clear vision which reveal a subtler state of being, and which lift the fog, letting in "the glory which never was on sea or land." Dr. Bennett of Yale expresses these ideas in very beautiful terms. He says:

"A film falls from the eyes and the world appears in a new light. Things are no longer ordinary. There comes the certainty that *this* is the real world whose true character human blindness has until now concealed.

> Not where the wheeling systems darken
> And our benumbed conceiving soars;—
> The drift of pinions, would we harken,
> Beats at our own clay-shuttered doors.
> The angels keep their ancient places;
> Turn but a stone and start a wing!
> 'Tis ye, 'tis your estrangèd faces
> That miss the many-splendoured thing.

"The experience is at first tantalizing, alluring. There is a rumor of a new world and the spirit is eager for the voyage upon strange seas. The familiar world must be left behind. The great adventure of religion begins. . . .

"There must somewhere be a point of certainty. A growing universe may provide for open futures, but whoso declares that the universe is growing states an unalterable fact about its structure, which fact is the eternal guarantee of the possibility and validity of experiment. . . .

"Man is a bridge. Even the superman, once we perceive that he is only the symbol of the strenuous ideal, turns out to be a bridge too. Our only assurance is that the gates of the future are always open."[7]

Perhaps the problem consists in this: that the gates of the future seem to open upon an immaterial world, and upon a realm that is intangible, metaphysical, supersensuous. We have well-nigh exhausted the resources of the material world, but we have not yet learned to function in a non-material one. We even deny its existence at times. We face the inevitable experience, which we call death, and yet take no rational steps to ascertain whether there really is a life beyond. The progress of evolution has produced a wonderful race, equipped with a sensitive response apparatus and a reasoning mind. We possess the rudiments of a sense which we call the intuition and, with this equipment, we stand before the gates of the future and ask the question: "To what purpose shall we put this composite, complex mechanism which we call a human being?" Have we reached our full development? Are there shades of meaning to life which have hitherto escaped our attention, and have they escaped our attention because we have latent powers and capacities as yet

[7] Bennett, Charles A., *A Philosophical Study of Mysticism*, pp. 23, 117, 130.

unrealized? Is it possible that we are blind to a vast world of life and of beauty, with its own appropriate laws and phenomena? Mystics, seers and thinkers of all ages and in both hemispheres have said such a world exists.

With this equipment, which we might call the personality, man stands with the past behind him, in a present that is full of chaos, and before a future into which he cannot look. He cannot stand still. He must go forward, and the vast educational, scientific, philosophic and religious organizations are all doing their utmost to tell him which way to go and to present to him a solution of his problem.

That which is static and crystallized eventually falls to pieces and, where there is arrested growth, abnormalities will occur and retrogression be found. Someone has said that the danger which we must avoid is that of a "disintegrating personality." If humanity is not potential, if man has reached his zenith and can go no further, then he should recognize this fact and make his decline and fall as easy and as beautiful as possible. It is encouraging to note how in 1850 the dim outlines of that portal into the New Age were vaguely seen and how much concern thinkers then evinced that man should not fail to learn his lesson and go forward. Read the words of Carlyle and note how appropriate they are to the present time.

"In the days that are passing over us, even fools are arrested to ask the meaning of them; few of the generations of men have seen more impressive days. Days of endless

calamity, disruption, dislocation, confusion worse confounded. . . . It is not a small hope that will suffice us, the
ruin being clearly . . . universal. There must be a new
world if there is to be a world at all. That human beings in
Europe can ever return to the old sorry routine, and proceed with any steadiness or continuance therein,—this small
hope is not now a tenable one. These days of universal death
must be days of universal rebirth, if the ruin is not to be
total and final. It is a time to make the dullest man consider whence he came and whither he is bound."[8]

Looking back over the seventy or more years that
have elapsed since Carlyle wrote these words, we
know that mankind did not fail to go forward. The
electrical age was inaugurated and the wonders of
the scientific achievements of our time are known by
us all. With optimism, therefore, in a time of fresh
crisis, we can go forward with true courage, for the
portals into the New Age are far more clearly seen.
Perhaps it is true also that man is only now attain-
ing his majority and is about to enter upon his in-
heritance and to discover within himself powers and
capacities, faculties and tendencies which are the
guarantee of a vital and useful manhood, and of
eternal existence. We are completing the stage
wherein the emphasis has been laid upon the mechanism, upon the sum-total of cells, which constitute
the body and the brain, with their automatic reaction
to pleasure, to pain and to thought. We know much
about Man, the machine. The mechanistic school of
psychologists have placed us deeply in their debt

⁸ Jacks, L. P., *Religious Perplexities*, p. 46.

with their discoveries about the apparatus whereby a human being comes into contact with his environment. But there are *men* among us, men who are not mere machines. We have the right to measure our ultimate capacities and our potential greatness by the achievements of the best among us; these great ones are not "freak" products of divine caprice or of blind evolutionary urge, but are themselves the guarantee of the ultimate achievement of the whole.

Irving Babbitt remarks, that there is a something in man's nature "that sets him apart simply as man, from other animals, and that something Cicero defines as a 'sense of order and decorum and measure in deeds and words'."[9] Babbitt adds (and this is the point to note) that "the world would have been a better place if more persons had made sure they were human before setting out to be superhuman."[10] There is, perhaps, an intermediate stage wherein we function as men, sustain our human relations, and discharge our just obligations, thus fulfilling our temporary destiny. The question arises here as to whether such a stage is even yet generally possible when we remember that there are millions of illiterate persons on our planet at this time!

But, along with this tendency toward pure humanity and the drift away from the standardization of the human unit, there emerges a group to whom we give the name of mystics. They testify to another world of experience and contacts. They bear witness

[9] Babbitt, Irving, *Humanism: An Essay at Definition.*
[10] *Ibid.*

to a personal realization and to a phenomenal manifestation and satisfaction of which the average man knows nothing. As Dr. Bennett says "the mystics themselves have described their attainment as a seeing into the meaning of the universe, a seeing of how all things belong together. They have found the clue."[11] Down the ages they have come forth and said in unison: there is another kingdom in nature. This kingdom has its own laws, its own phenomena and its own intimate relationships. It is the kingdom of the spirit. We have found it and you too can ascertain its nature. These witnesses fall into two groups; the purely mystical and emotional quester who sees the vision and falls down in an illuminated rapture before the beauty that he has sensed, and secondly, the knowers, who have added to the emotional rapture an intellectual achievement (an orientation of the mind) which enables them to do more than sense and enjoy. They understand; they know, and have become identified with that new world of being towards which the pure mystic reaches. The line of demarcation between these knowers of divine things and those who sense the vision is very slight.

There is, however, a no-man's ground between the two groups on which a great transition takes place. There is an interlude in experience and in development which changes the visionary mystic into the practical knower. There is a process and a technique to which the mystic can subject himself which coordinates him and develops in him a new and subtle

[11] Bennett, Charles A., *A Philosophical Study of Mysticism*, p. 81.

apparatus, by means of which he no longer *sees* the vision of divine reality but knows himself to be that reality itself. It is with this transitional process and with this work of educating the mystic, that the meditation technique has to do. It is this with which we deal in this book.

The problem of leading man into his heritage as a human being is the function of the educators and of the psychologists. They must lead him up to the door of the mystical world. Paradoxical as it may sound, the work of leading him into his spiritual heritage is the work of religion and of science. Dr. Pupin tells us that "science and religion supplement each other, they are the two pillars of the portal through which the human soul enters into the world where divinity resides."[12]

Let us give the word "spiritual" a wide connotation! I do not here speak of religious truths; the formulations of the theologians and the churchmen in all the big religious organizations, both Eastern and Western, may, or may not, be true. Let us use the word "spiritual" to signify the world of light and beauty, of order and of purpose, about which the world Scriptures speak, which is the object of the attentive research of the scientists, and into which the pioneers of the human family have always penetrated, returning to tell us of their experiences. Let us regard all manifestations of life as spiritual, and so widen the usual meaning of this word to signify

[12] Pupin, Michael, *The New Reformation*, p. 217.

the energies and potencies which lie back of every form in nature and which give to each of them their essential distinguishing characteristics and qualities. For thousands of years all over the planet, the mystics and knowers have borne witness to experiences in subtler worlds where they have been brought into contact with forces and phenomena which are not of this physical world. They speak of meeting with angelic hosts; they refer to the great cloud of witnesses; they commune with the elder brothers of the race who work in other dimensions and who demonstrate powers about which ordinary human beings know nothing; they speak of a light and of a glory; of a direct knowledge of truth and of a world of phenomena which is uniform to the mystics of all races. That much of the testimony can be discarded on the grounds of hallucination may be true; that many of the saints of old were psychopathic cases and neurotics may be equally true; but there still remains a residue of testimony and a sufficient number of reputable witnesses, substantiating this testimony, to force our belief in its verity. These witnesses to the unseen world spoke with words of power and gave forth messages which have moulded the thoughts of men, and directed the lives of millions. They claimed there was a science of spiritual knowledge and a technique of development whereby men could attain to the mystical experience and whereby they could know God.

It is this science which we will study in this book,

and this technique which we will seek to unfold. It deals with the right use of the mind, whereby the world of souls reveals itself and that secret door is found and opened which leads from darkness to light, from death to immortality and from the unreal to the Real.

The ultimate solution of our world problem lies in our arrival at this knowledge—a knowledge that is neither eastern nor western, but which is known to both. When we have joined hands with the Orient and when we have united the best thoughts of the East with those of the West, we shall have a synthetic and balanced teaching which will liberate the coming generations. It must begin in the educational field and with the young.

In the West, consciousness has been focused upon the material aspects of living, and all of our mental power has been concentrated upon the control and utilization of material things, the perfecting of physical comforts, and the accumulation of possessions. In the East, where the spiritual realities have been more uniformly held, mental power has been used in concentration and meditation and in deep philosophical and metaphysical study, but the masses of the people, not capable of these activities, have been left in peculiar and strikingly terrible conditions, from the standpoint of physical living. Through the blending of the achievements of the two civilizations (now going on with increasing rapidity) a balance is being struck by means of which the race

as a whole will be able to demonstrate its full potency. Both the East and the West are gradually
learning to take from each other to mutual advan-
tage, and work in this field is one of the fundamental
and necessary things of the present cycle.

Chapter Two

THE PURPOSE OF EDUCATION

". . . education is undergoing important transformations. From a relatively external process of pouring in facts, it is increasingly becoming a process of evoking the deeper, generative possibilities that lie within the individual."

H. A. OVERSTREET

THE PURPOSE OF EDUCATION

ONE of the many factors which have brought humanity to its present point of development has been the growth and perfecting of its educational methods and systems. At first this was in the hands of the organized religions, but now it is practically divorced from the control of the religious bodies, and lies in the hands of the state. In the past, education was largely colored by theology and its methods were dictated by the churchmen and the priests. Now the vast body of teachers are trained by the state; any religious bias is ignored on account of the many differentiated religious bodies, and the trend of the teaching is almost entirely materialistic and scientific. In the past, both in the East and in the West, we have had the education of the more highly evolved members of the human family. Today we have mass education. In approaching any understanding of the future and (we believe) higher education, these two facts must be borne in mind for it will be in a synthesis of these two methods—individual and mass education—religious and scientific—that the way out will be found.

Like everything else in this transitional period, our educational systems are in a state of flux and of change. A general feeling that much has been done to raise the level of the human mind is everywhere to be found, coupled with a deep undercurrent of dissatisfaction with the results. We are questioning whether our educational systems *are* achieving the widest good. We appreciate the enormous advance that has been made during the past two hundred years, and yet we wonder whether we are, after all, getting as much out of life as should be possible to people with an adequate system of training. We are smugly satisfied with our growth in knowledge, our accumulation of information, and our control of the forces of nature, and yet we hold collegiate debates as to whether we have any true culture. We teach our children to memorize an enormous array of facts, and to assimilate a vast amount of widely diversified detail, and yet we question sometimes whether we are teaching them to live more satisfactorily. We use billions of dollars to build and endow universities and colleges and yet our most far-sighted educators are gravely concerned as to whether this organized education is really meeting the needs of the average citizen. It certainly seems to fail in its mission with the unusual child and with the gifted man or woman. Our mode of training our youth is standing decidedly before the bar of judgment. Only the future can settle whether some way out will not have to be found whereby the culture of the individual can proceed alongside the civilizing, through education, of the masses.

In an age of scientific achievement and of a synthesis of thought in every department of human knowledge, one of our educators, Dr. Rufus M. Jones says:

"But, alas, none of these achievements makes us better men. There is no equation between bank accounts and goodness of heart. Knowledge is by no means the same thing as wisdom or nobility of spirit. . . . The world has never seen before such an immense army of educators at work on the youth of the country, nor has there ever been before in the history of the world, such a generous outlay of money for education, both lower and higher. The total effect, however, is disappointing, and misses the central point. Our institutions of learning produce some good scholars and give a body of scientific facts to a great number. But there is a pitiable failure in the main business of education which is, or should be, the formation of character, the culture of the spirit, the building of the soul."[1]

Old Mother Asia and Europe, up to the eighteenth century, trained and cultured the individual. An intensified training was given to the so-called upper classes, and to the man who showed a marked aptitude for spiritual culture. Under the Brahmanical system in the East, and in the monasteries in the West, a specialized culture was imparted to those who could profit by it, and rare individuals were produced, who, to this day, set their mark upon human thought. For this our modern Occidental world has substituted mass education. For the first time, men in their thousands are being taught to use their minds; they are beginning to assert their own indi-

[1] Jones, Rufus M., *The Need for a Spiritual Element in Education.* World Unity Magazine, October, 1928.

vidualities, and to formulate their own ideas. The freedom of human thought, liberation from the control of theologies (religious or scientific) are the war cries of the present, and much has thereby been gained. The masses are beginning to do their own thinking. But it is largely mass thinking, and haphazard public opinion now moulds thought just as much as theologies formerly did. The pioneering individual has still as much difficulty in making himself felt in the present world of thought and of endeavor, as of old.

Perhaps in the turning of the great wheel of life, we are due again to revert to the ancient method of specialized training for the special individual—a reversion which will not involve a discarding of mass education. In this way, we may ultimately unify the methods of the past and of the East with those of the present and of the West.

Before considering these two methods let us attempt to define education, to express to ourselves its goal and so clarify our ideas as to the objectives ahead of all our endeavor.

This is no easy thing to do. Viewed from its most uninteresting aspect, education can briefly be defined as the imparting of knowledge to a student, and usually to an unwilling student, who receives a mass of information that does not interest him in the least. A note of dryness and of aridity is struck; we feel that this presentation deals primarily with memory training, with the impartation of so-called facts, and with giving the student a little information on a vast number of unrelated subjects. The literal meaning of the word, however, is "to lead out of," or "to draw out," and this is most instructive. The thought latent in this idea is that we should draw out the inherent instincts and potentialities of the child in order to lead him out of one state of consciousness into another and wider one. In this way we lead children, for instance, who are simply conscious of being alive, into a state of self-consciousness; they become aware of themselves and of their group relationships; they are taught to develop powers and capacities, especially through vocational training, in order that they may be economically independent, and thus self-supporting members of society. We exploit their instinct of self-preservation in order to lead them on along the path of knowledge. Could it be said that we begin with the utilization of their instinctive apparatus to lead them on to the way of the intellect? Perhaps this may be true, but I question whether, having brought them thus far we carry on the good work and teach them the real meaning of intellection as a training whereby the intuition is released. We teach them to utilize their instincts and intellect as part of the apparatus of self-preservation in the external world of human affairs, but the use of pure reason and the eventual control of the mind by the intuition in the work of self-preservation and of continuity of consciousness in the subjective and real worlds, is as yet but the privileged knowledge of a few pioneers.

If Professor H. Wildon Carr is right, in his definition of the intuition, then our educational methods do not tend to its development. He defines it as "the apprehension by the mind of reality directly as it is, and not under the form of a perception or a conception, nor as an idea or object of the reason, all of which by contrast are intellectual apprehension."[2]

We rate the science of the mind or the modifications of the thinking principle (as the Hindu calls it) as strictly human, relegating man's instinctual reactions to qualities he shares in common with the animals. May it not be possible that the science of the intuition, the art of clear synthetic vision, may some day stand to the intellect as it, in its turn, stands to the instinctual faculty.

Dr. Dibblee of Oxford makes the following interesting comments upon instinct and intuition, which have their place here on account of our plea in this book for the recognition of an educational technique which would lead to the development of a faculty of a higher awareness. He says:

". . . both instinct and intuition begin within the extra-conscious parts of ourselves, to speak in a local figure, and emerge equally unexpectedly into the light of every day consciousness. . . . The impulses of instinct and the promptings of intuition are engendered in total secrecy. When they do appear, they are necessarily almost complete, and their advent into our consciousness is sudden."[3]

[2] Carr, H. Wildon, *Philosophy of Change*, p. 21.
[3] Dibblee, George Binney, *Instinct and Intuition*. p. 128.

And he adds in another place that intuition lies on the other side of reason to instinct. We have, therefore, this interesting triplicity—instinct, intellect and intuition—with instinct lying below the threshold of consciousness, so to speak, with the intellect holding the first place in the recognition of man, as human, and with the intuition lying beyond both of them, and only occasionally making its presence felt in the sudden illuminations and apprehensions of truth which are the gift of our greatest thinkers.

Surely there must be something more to the educational process than just fitting a man to cope with external facts and with his arbitrary environment? Humanity must be led out and into a deeper and wider future and realization. It must be equipped to meet and handle whatever may come, so as to get the highest and the best results. Men's powers should be drawn out to their fullest constructive expression. There must be no standardized limit of achievement, the attainment of which will leave them complacent, self-satisfied and, therefore, static. They must always be led from lower to higher states of realization, and the faculty of awareness must be steadily expanded. Expansion and growth is the law of life and while the mass of men must be lifted by a system of education, fitted to bring the greatest good to the greatest number, the individual must be given his full heritage, and special culture provided which will foster and strengthen the finest and the best amongst us, for in their achievement lies the

promise of the New Age. The inferior and the back-
ward must also have special training in order that
they may come up to the high standard which the
educators set. But it is of even greater importance
that no man, with a special aptitude and equipment,
should be held down to the dead level of the mass
standard of the educated class.

It is right here that the difficulty of defining education becomes apparent, and the questions arise as
to the real goal and the true objectives. Dr. Randall
realizes this in an article he wrote, in which he says:

"I would like to recommend the defining of education as
a possible exercise for private meditation. Let each one ask
himself what he means by 'education'; and if he ponders
the question deeply he will discover that in order to answer
it he will have to probe down to the innermost meaning of
life itself. Thinking earnestly about the meaning of education compels us to face the fundamental questions of life
as we never have before. . . . Is the goal of education
knowledge? Assuredly yes, but knowledge for what? Is its
goal power? Again yes, but power to what end? Is its goal
social adjustment? The modern age replies emphatically,
yes, but what kind of adjustment shall it be, and determined by what ideals? That education aims not at mere
knowledge or mere power of any kind, but at knowledge
and power put to right uses is clearly recognized by the
most progressive educational thought, though not by the
popular opinion of the day. . . .

"The new education has for its great end, therefore, the
training and development of the individual for social ends,
that is, for the largest service to man. . . .

"We commonly classify education under three heads—
primary, secondary and higher. To these three I should like

to add a fourth, *highest*. The highest education is religion but it is also education."[4]

It is interesting to note that the same ideas are expressed by Bhagavān Dās at the First All-Asia Educational Conference. He says:

"The rules of Religion, i.e., of the larger Science, enable us . . . to discharge all these wider debts and duties. Religion has been described as the command or revelation of God. This only means, in other words, the laws of God's Nature, as revealed to us by the labours, intellectual, intuitional, inspirational, of the seers and scientists of all religions and all nations. . . . We have heard of the three R's long enough. This fourth R, of genuine Religion, is more important than them all. . . . But it has to be carefully discovered and thought out first. It behooves all sincere educators to help in this work by applying the scientific method of ascertaining agreements amidst differences."[5]

Both East and West seem to feel that an educational system that does not eventually lead a man out of the world of human affairs into the wider consciousness of spiritual things has failed in its mission and will not measure up to the soaring demand of the human soul. A training that stops short with the intellect, and ignores the faculty to intuit truth which the best minds evidence, lacks much. If it leaves its students with closed and static minds, it has left them without the equipment to touch that intangible and finest "four-fifths of life" which Dr. Wiggam tells us, lies outside the realm of scientific

[4] Randall, John Herman, *Education and Religion,* World Unity Magazine, October, 1928.

[5] Dās, Bhagavān, *The Unity of Asiatic Thought, i.e., Of All Religions,* p. 12.

training altogether.[6] The door must be opened for those who can go beyond the academic training of the mind with relation to physical plane living.

The success of the future of the race is bound up with the success of those individuals who have the capacity to achieve greater, because more spiritual, things. These units of the human family must be discovered and encouraged to go on and to penetrate into the realm of the intangible. They must be cultured and trained and given an education which will be adapted to the highest and the best that is in them. Such an education requires a proper perception of individual growth and status, and a right understanding of what the next step in any given case should be. It requires insight, sympathy and understanding on the part of the teacher.

There is an increasing realization among educators of this need to lift the more advanced educational processes and so raise those subjected to their influence out of the realm of the purely analytical critical mind into that of pure reason and intuitive perception. Bertrand Russell points out that ''Education should not aim at a passive awareness of dead facts but at an activity directed towards the world that our efforts are to create.'' But we must remember that creation posits an alive and functioning creator, acting with intention and utilizing the creative imagination. Could it be said that this is the effect of our modern educational systems? Is not the mind standardized and held down by our mass sys-

⁶ Wiggam, Albert Edward, *The New Decalogue of Science.*

tem and by the method of cramming the memory with ill digested facts? If Herbart is right when he says that the "chief business of education is the ethical revelation of the universe" then perhaps Dr. Moran is also right when he points out that "one of the underlying causes, perhaps the greatest, of our materialistic age is the lack of the spiritual element in our formal education."

Some of us feel also that there exists an even wider goal than an ethical revelation; and that it is possible that humanity is the custodian of an illumination and a glory which will only be realized in its fulness when the masses achieve some of the magnificence which has characterized the World Figures of the past. Is it not in line with evolutionary development that the real goal of education is *to lead humanity out of the fourth or human kingdom into that spiritual realm* where the pioneers whom we call Mystics, and the standard-setting Figures of the race live and move and have their being? Thus mankind will be raised out of the objective material world into the realm of spirit, where the truer values are to be found, and wherein that larger Self is contacted which the individual selves exist only to reveal. Keyserling hints at this in the following words:

"We are aware of the limits of human reason; we understand the significance of our striving; we are the masters of nature. We can simultaneously overlook the inner and the outer world. Since we can scientifically determine what are our real intentions, we need no more become the prey of self-deceptions. . . . From now on, this possibility must become the *conscious* motive of life. Hitherto it has not yet played that part. Yet this precisely is all-important for the centre of consciousness determines the starting-point of man. Wherever he shifts the emphasis within himself, there it actually rests; the whole Being of man is reorganized accordingly . . . therefore, an education to the synthesis of understanding and action is necessary for a life based on recognition.

"All education in the East is purely directed towards Sense-understanding, which . . . is the only way that can be shown as leading to a raising of the level of essential Being. . . . *The essential thing is not information, but understanding,* and understanding can be attained only by personal creative application. . . . Sense-perception always means *giving a thing a meaning*; the dimension of Significance lies in the direction from within to the outside. Therefore, knowledge (in the sense of information) and understanding in reality, bear the same relationship to each other as nature and Spirit. Information is gained from without to the inside; understanding is a creative process in the opposite direction. Under these circumstances, there is no direct way leading from one goal to the other. One may know everything without at the same time understanding anything at all. And that is precisely the pass to which our education, that aims at a hoarding of information, has brought the majority."[8]

This book seeks to deal with the method whereby the capacity to function in the larger consciousness can be developed, and man can re-organize his Being towards the wider issues. It concerns itself with the technique by which a specialized training and self-culture can be applied by every individual unit who

[8] Keyserling, Count Hermann, *Creative Understanding*, pp. 257, 216, 217.

is capable of desiring this larger goal. If that desire can take a clear and rational form in his mind and can be appreciated as a perfectly legitimate objective, capable of successful achievement, he will eagerly grasp at it. If society can provide the means and opportunity for such advancement, many will gladly seek the way. The method proposed is an individual technique which will enable the student, who has profited by the usual academic educational advantages and the experiences of life, to expand his consciousness until he gradually transcends his present limitations and reorients his mind to wider realizations. He will discover the soul as the great Reality, thus gaining direct experience of spiritual things.

Everett Dean Martin defines education for us as a "spiritual revaluation of human life. Its task is to *reorient* the individual, to enable him to take a richer and more significant view of his experiences, to place him above and not within the system of his beliefs and ideals.'"[9] This definition necessarily opens the door to controversy, for we live, each of us, in a different environment; we have each our special problems and characteristics, based upon our heredity, our physical condition and many other factors. The consequent standard of values will have to be modified for each person, for each generation, country and race. That education is intended to prepare us for "complete living" (as Herbert Spencer

[9] Martin, Everett Dean, *The Meaning of a Liberal Education*, p. viii, Preface.

says) may be true, but the scope and capacity of each man differs. The lowest and the highest attainable point for men varies infinitely, and a man, moreover, who is equipped to function in one particular sphere might prove ludicrously inadequate in another. Some standard of "complete living" must therefore be worked out if the definition is to be useful. To do this we shall have to ascertain what is the pure type of the rounded out and perfected man, and what is the sum total of his range of contacts. It does not seem possible that we have exhausted the possibilities of man's response apparatus, nor of the environment with which it can put him in touch. What are the limits within which man can function? If there are states of awareness, ranging all the way from that of the Hottentot up to that of our intelligentsia and on to the geniuses and leaders in all fields of human expression, what constitutes the difference between them? Why are their fields of perception so widely diverse? Racial development, one will reply; glandular stability, or instability, another will say; the possession, or the lack, of adequate educational advantages, differences in environment and in heritage, other groups of thinkers will decide.

But out of the welter of opinion emerges the basic fact of the wide range of the human states of awareness, and the wonder of the realization that humanity has produced such marvels of comprehensive understanding, of purity of expression and of perfected world-wide influence as we see evidenced by the Christ, the Buddha, Plato and many others, whose thoughts and words have set their mark upon the minds of men for thousands of years. What has made them what they are? Are they miracles, emerging from the heart of the Infinite, and, hence, can never find their equal? Are they products of the evolutionary process, and so have become potent through vast experience and unfoldment? Or are they the flower of the human race, who added to their equipment and training a specialized culture which enabled them to enter a spiritual world, which is sealed to the majority, and to function in a dimension of which even our most advanced thinkers know nothing? Have our present educational systems brought humanity, as a whole, to a condition where many thousands are ready for this specialized culture, and, therefore, are we facing a crisis in the educational field which has its roots in a success, which, if carried forward along the same lines, will become a detriment instead of a help,—because man is ready for something new? Some of us believe that this is possible, and that it is time that educators should begin to prepare men for the new and divine experience and for that wonderful experiment which will put them everywhere in possession of themselves—a thing hitherto the choice prerogative of the mystics and knowers of the race. These knowers have testified to a wider world than the one revealed to us by the mechanism of the nerves, and investigated by the chemist, the physicist, the biologist and the anthropologist. They have spoken in no un-

certain terms of a realm of contacts and of awareness in which the ordinary senses are useless. They
claim to have lived and moved in these subtler
realms, and the perseverance displayed in the
mystical search for reality, and the similarity of
their testimony down the ages lead one to believe in
the possibility of that intangible world and of a response apparatus, by means of which it can be contacted. The ranks of these ''deluded'' mystics and
intuitional thinkers number tens of thousands of the
best minds of the race. They say to us in the words
of Walt Whitman: ''I and my kind do not convince
by argument; we convince by our presence.''[10]

Education has also been expressed as ''an adventurous quest for the meaning of life, involving an
ability to think things through.'' Who said this I do
not know, but it seems to me a most excellent description of the way of the mystic and the technique
of meditation whereby the mystic becomes the fully
conscious knower. However much one may seek to
explain it away, the fact remains that man goes
questing through the ages, and his quest leads him
far deeper than the concrete externals of the world
in which he lives. Dr. Overstreet calls this to our attention in words that carry the true mystical message. He says:

''In the main, we are creatures who see 'things'. We see
what we see and usually not beyond what we see. To experience the world as merely a world of things is doubtless
to fail of something that is significant. The experience of

[10] Whitman, Walt, *Leaves of Grass.*

things, to be sure, is good as far as it goes. It enables us to move about our world and to manipulate the life-factors with some success. . . . It is possible, however, to get a different 'feel' of one's world if one is able to develop another habit of mind. It is, in short, the habit of seeing the invisible in the visible reality; the habit of penetrating surfaces, of seeing through things to their initiating sources.''[11]

Men are now perhaps ready to penetrate beneath the surface and to carry their search within the outer form of nature to that which is its cause. We are perhaps, too apt to confuse the religious spirit with the mystic search. All clear thinking about life and about the great laws of nature, if carried forward with persistence and steadfastness, leads eventually into the mystic world, and this the foremost scientists of our day are beginning to realize. Religion starts with the accepted hypothesis of the unseen and the mystical. But science arrives at the same point by working from the seen to the unseen and from the objective to the subjective. Thus, as has been said, by the process of investigation and of passing inwards from form to form, the mystic arrives eventually at the glory of the unveiled Self. It seems to be unalterably true that all paths lead to God—viewing God as the ultimate goal, the symbol of man's search for Reality. It is no longer a sign of superstition to believe in a higher dimension and in another world of Being. Even the word "supernatural" has become deeply and profoundly respectable, and it seems possible that some day our

[11] Overstreet, H. A., *The Enduring Quest*, p. 114.

educational systems may regard the preparation of the individual to transcend his natural limitations as an entirely legitimate part of its affairs. It is interesting to note what Dr. C. Lloyd Morgan in the Gifford Lectures, delivered in 1923, has to say about this word "supernatural." He says:

"There is, I submit, an intelligible sense in which it may be said that, in the ascending hierarchy of stages of progress, regarded as manifestations of Divine Purpose, each higher stage is in turn *super*natural to that which precedes it. In this sense life is supernatural to the inorganic; reflective comprehension in thought is supernatural to naive unreflective perception; the religious attitude, with acknowledgement of Divine Purpose, is supernatural to the ethical attitude in social affairs. For those who reach this highest stage, as they deem it, the religious attitude affords the supreme exemplar of the supernatural. It is distinctive of the spiritual man."[12]

and, he adds most beautifully and most appositely, as far as our subject is concerned, that "The stress for us is on a new *attitude*, for it is this that is, as I think, emergent. Hence we may speak of a new 'vision,' and a new 'heart,' capable of a higher and richer form of joy."[13]

In Dr. Hocking's notable book *"Human Nature and Its Remaking"* he points out that education has two functions. It must first of all communicate the type and then provide for growth beyond that type. Education is intended to make man truly human; it must round out and perfect his nature, and so reveal

[12] Morgan, C. Lloyd, *Life, Mind and Spirit*, p. X, Preface.
[13] *Ibid.*

and make possible those deeper potentialities towards which all humanity tends. The evocation of the will-to-know, and, later, of the will-to-be, must follow a natural process of development. It is in this connection that the method of meditation will be seen as a part of the technique of the higher education which the New Age will see developed; it will be found to be the means whereby the rounded out human being can be still further developed, and led forth into a new kingdom in nature. Meditation is primarily a self-initiated process of education, calling forth all the powers of the will, basing itself upon the equipment present, but producing at the end a new type, the soul type, with its own internal apparatus, and holding within itself again the seeds of still greater unfoldment.

From being something imposed from without, the new educational process wells up from within, and becomes that self-imposed mental discipline, which we cover by those much misunderstood words—concentration, meditation, and contemplation. From being a process of memory training, and the development of a quick handling of the response apparatus which puts us in touch with the external world, the educational technique becomes a system of mind-control, leading eventually to an inner awareness of a new state of being. It produces at length a rapid re-action and responsiveness to a world, intangible and unseen, and to a new series of instinctual recognitions which have their seat in a subtler response apparatus. The soul type imposes itself upon the human type, as the human has done upon the animal, and just as the human type is the product of mass training and instinct and has been tremendously unfolded by our modern educational systems, so the soul type is the product of a new method of mental training, imposed on the individual by his soul, and called forth by the urgency of the quest and by the act of his will. This soul is always latent in the human form, but is drawn into demonstrated activity through the practice of meditation.

These two methods of rounding out the human being and raising him to a mass standard, and of producing the emergence of the new type, the soul, constitute the main distinction between the western and eastern educational methods.

The contrast between the two ways of development is most instructive. In the East we have the careful culture of the individual, with the masses left practically without any education. In the West we have mass education, but the individual is left, speaking generally, without any specific culturing. These two great and divergent systems have each produced a civilization, expressing its peculiar genius and manifestations, but also its marked defects. The premises upon which the systems are based are widely divergent, and it would be worth our while to consider them, for in understanding them and in the eventual union of the two it is possible that the way out may be found for the new race in the New Age.

First: In the eastern system, it is assumed that

within every human form dwells an entity, a being, called the self or soul. Second: This self utilizes the form of the human being as its instrument or means of expression, and through the sum total of the mental and emotional states will eventually manifest itself, utilizing the physical body as its functioning mechanism on the physical plane. Finally, the control of these means of expression is brought about under the Law of Rebirth. Through the evolutionary process (carried forward through many lives in a physical body) the self gradually builds a fit instrument through which to manifest, and learns to master it. Thus the self or soul becomes truly creative and self-conscious in the highest sense and active in its environment, manifesting its true nature perfectly. Eventually it gains complete liberation from form, from the thralldom of the desire nature, and the domination of the intellect. This final emancipation, and consequent transfer of the centre of consciousness from the human to the spiritual kingdom, is hastened and nurtured by a specialized education, called the meditation process, which is superimposed upon a mind widely and wisely cultured.

The result of this intensive and individual training has been spectacular in the extreme. The eastern method is the only one which has produced the Founders of all the world religions, for all are Asiatic in origin. It is responsible for the appearance of those inspired Scriptures of the world which have moulded the thoughts of men, and for the coming forth of all the world Saviours—the Buddha, Zoroaster, Shri Krishna, the Christ, and others. Thus the East has manifested forth, as the result of its particular technique, all the Great Individuals, who have sounded the note for their particular age, given the needed teaching for the unfoldment in the minds of men of the God-Idea, and so led humanity forward along the path of spiritual perception. The exoteric result of their lives is to be seen in the great organized religions.

In the training of the highly developed individuals, however, the masses throughout Asia have been neglected, and the system, consequently, (from the angle of racial development), leaves much to be desired. The defects of the system are the development of visionary and impractical tendencies. The mystic is frequently unable to cope with his environment, and where the emphasis is laid entirely upon the subjective side of life, the physical welfare of the individual and the race is neglected and overlooked. The masses are left to struggle in the mire of ignorance, disease and dirt, and, hence, we have the deplorable conditions found throughout the Orient, alongside the highest spiritual illumination of the favored few.

In the West the emphasis is entirely reversed. The subjective is ignored and regarded as hypothetical, and the premises upon which our culture is based are as follows: First, there is an entity, called the human being, who possesses a mind, a set of emotions and a response apparatus through which he is brought into contact with his environment. Second, according to the calibre of his apparatus and the condition of his mind, plus the nature of his environing circumstances, so will be his character and disposition. The goal of the educational process, applied wholesale and indiscriminately, is to make him physically fit, mentally alert, to provide a trained memory, controlled reactions, and a character which makes him a social asset and a contributing factor in the body economic. His mind is regarded as a storehouse for imparted facts and the training given every child is intended to make him a useful member of society, self-supporting and decent. The product of these premises is the reverse of the Oriental. We have no specific culture of a kind to produce such world figures as Asia has produced, but we have evolved a mass system of education, and we have developed groups of thinkers. Hence, our universities, colleges and public and private schools. These set their mark upon tens of thousands of men, standardizing them and training them so that we turn out a human product, possessing a certain uniform knowledge, a certain stereotyped store of facts and a smattering of information. This means that there is no such deplorable ignorance as we find in the East, but a fairly high level of general knowledge. It has produced what we call civilization, with its wealth of books, and its many sciences. It has produced the scientific investigation of man, and (on the crest of the wave of human evolution) the great Groups in contradistinction to the great Individuals.

The contrasts might be crudely summed up as follows:

WEST	EAST
Groups	Individuals
Books	Bibles
Knowledge	Wisdom
Objective Civilization	Subjective Culture
Mechanical Development	Mystical Development
Standardization	Uniqueness
Mass Education	Specialized Training
Science	Religion
Memory Training	Meditation
Investigation	Reflection

Yet the cause is basically one—a method of education. Both are also fundamentally right, yet both are needed to supplement and complement each other. The education of the masses of the Orient will lead to the rectifying of their physical plane problems which call aloud for solution. A wide general system of education reaching down among the illiterate masses of the people in Asia is the outstanding need. The culturing of the individual in the West, and the grafting upon his body of imposed knowledge, of a technique of Soul Culture, as it has come to us from the Orient, will lift and salvage our civilization which is so fast breaking down. The East needs knowledge and the imparting of information. The West needs wisdom and the technique of meditation.

This scientific and cultural system, when applied to our highly educated human beings, will produce that bridging body of men, who will unify the achievements of the two hemispheres and link the subjective and objective realms. They will act as the pioneers of the New Age, when men will be practical men of affairs with their feet firmly planted on earth and yet, at the same time, be mystics and seers, living also in the world of spirit and carrying inspiration and illumination with them into the life of every day.

For the bringing about of these conditions and the production of that great group of practical mystics who will eventually save the world, two things are needed:—trained minds with wide general knowledge as a foundation (and this our western system can give), plus a spiritual awareness of the indwelling divinity, the soul, to be achieved through the eastern system of scientific meditation. Our greatest need in the West lies in our failure to recognize the Soul and the faculty of the intuition which in its turn leads to illumination. The late Professor Luzzatti, Prime Minister of Italy, in the Preface to his most valuable and scholarly book *"God and Freedom"* says: "It is everywhere noticed that the growth of the empire of man over himself does not keep step with the growth of the empire of man over nature."[14] It is essential that the western world should perfect its educational systems in such a way as to bring about this conquest of the empire of ourselves.

[14] Luzzatti, Luigi, *God and Freedom*.

CHAPTER THREE

THE NATURE OF THE SOUL

"Philosophers say the Soul is double-faced, her upper face gazes at God all the time and her lower face looks somewhat down, informing the senses; and the upper face, which is the summit of the soul, is in eternity and has nothing to do with time: it knows nothing of time or of body."

MEISTER ECKHART

The Nature of the Soul

IN DETAILING the technique whereby it is claimed the educated intellectual can become the intuitional knower it might be well to state the hypotheses upon which the science of meditation is based. In the process the various aspects (in nature, or of divinity, whichever is preferred) of which man is the expression have to be recognized, but the basic connection which holds him together as an integrated unity must never be forgotten. Man is an integrated being, but existence means more to some men than to others. For some it is purely animal existence; for many it connotes the sum total of emotional and sensory experience; for others, it involves all this, plus a mental awareness which greatly enriches and deepens life. For a few (and those the flower of the human family) Being stands for a recognition of ability to register contacts that are universal and subjective as well as individual and objective. Keyserling says that:

"When we speak of the Being of a man in contradistinction to his ability, we mean his vital soul; and when we say this Being decides, we mean that all his utterances are penetrated with individual life, that every single expression

49

radiates personality, and that this personality is ultimately responsible."[1]

It might be stated here as *sine qua non* that only those people who are responsible thinking beings are ready for the application of those rules and instructions which will enable them to make that transition and to come to that consciousness which is the hallmark of the illuminated mystic and the intuitional knowers. The beautiful lines found in Dr. Winslow Hall's *Illuminanda* point the goal:

"In all men lurks The Light; yet, in how few
Has it blazed forth, as rightfully it ought,
Illuming, from within, our fleshly lamp,
And kindling cosmic flame in nigh-brought souls!
Splendour of God, how few! And ours the blame;
For, ever, crassly, by routine and wrath,
We undiscerningly damp down and choke
The spark of God that glints in every child.
All children are, by nature, bits of God;
And God, if they but had their freedom, would
Unfold Himself in them, would burgeon forth
Tinting and moulding, till, as perfect flowers
They bloomed, fulfilled of loveliness unveiled."[2]

This is the goal of the meditation process—to lead men forth into the Light that is within themselves and enable them, in that light, to see Light. This work of revelation is based on certain definite theories as to the constitution and nature of the human being. The evolution and perfecting of the mind faculty in man, with its keenness and capacity for

[1] Keyserling, Count Hermann, *Creative Understanding*, p. 180.
[2] Hall, W. Winslow, M.D., *Illuminanda*, p. 218.

concentration gives the West at this time the opportunity to put these theories to the test. An intelligent experiment is now naturally in order. "The new synthesis of mind and soul," Keyserling says, "must originate from the mind, on the height of supreme intellectuality, if something decisive is to happen."[3]

But to do this, there must be a clear understanding of three points upon which the Oriental position is based, and which, if true, validate the entire contention of the student of the Oriental technique of meditation, never forgetting, however, the proverb of the Chinese which says that, "If the wrong man uses the right means, the right means work in the wrong way." These three premises are:

First: There is a soul in every human form, and that soul uses the lower aspects of man simply as vehicles of expression. The objective of the evolutionary process is to enhance and deepen the control of the soul over this instrument. When this is complete, we have a divine incarnation.

Secondly: The sum total of these lower aspects, when developed and co-ordinated we call the Personality. This unity is composed of the mental and emotional states of being, the vital energy and the physical response apparatus, and these "mask" or hide the soul. These aspects develop sequentially and progressively, according to the eastern philosophy, and only on reaching a relatively high state of unfoldment does it become possible for man to

[3] Keyserling, Count Hermann, *Creative Understanding*, p. 125.

coordinate them and later to unify them, in consciousness, with the indwelling soul. Later comes control by the soul, and a steadily increasing expression of the nature of the soul. This is sometimes symbolically expressed as a light in a lamp. At first the lamp gives forth no radiance, but gradually the light makes its presence felt, till the meaning of the words of the Christ becomes clear. He said, "I am the light of the world," and enjoined upon His disciples to "let your light shine that man may see."

Thirdly: When the life of the soul, acting under the Law of Rebirth, has brought the personality to such a condition that it is an integrated and coordinated unit, then there is set up between the two a more intensive interaction. This interaction is brought about through the processes of self-discipline, an active will towards spiritual Being, unselfish service (for that is the mode in which the group-conscious soul manifests itself) and meditation. The consummation of the work is the conscious realization of union—called, in Christian terminology, the at-one-ment.

These three hypotheses must be accepted, at any rate, tentatively, if this process of education through meditation is to be rendered effective. In Webster's Dictionary, the soul is defined in line with these theories, and the definition runs as follows:

"An entity conceived as the essence, substance, or actuating cause of individual life, especially of life manifested in psychical activities; the vehicle of individual existence, separate in nature from the body and usually held to be separable in existence.''[4]

Webster adds the following comment which is appropriate in its application to our theme that "some conceptions, such as that of Fechner, that the soul is the whole unitary spiritual process in conjunction with the whole unitary bodily process, appear to stand midway between the idealistic and materialistic views.''[5] The strictly Oriental position is given us by Dr. Radhakrishnan, of the University of Calcutta, as follows:

"All organic beings have a principle of self-determination, to which the name of 'soul' is generally given. In the strict sense of the word, 'soul' belongs to every being that has life in it, and the different souls are fundamentally identical in nature. The differences are due to the physical organizations that obscure and thwart the life of the soul. The nature of the bodies in which the souls are incorporated accounts for their various degrees of obscuration. . . . The ego is the psychological unity of that stream of conscious experiencing which constitutes what we know as the inner life of an empirical self.

"The empirical self is the mixture of free spirit and mechanism, of purusa and prakriti. . . . Every ego possesses within the gross material body, which suffers dissolution at death, a subtle body, formed of the psychical apparatus, including the senses.''[6]

This soul, we are told, is a fragment of the Oversoul, a spark of the one Flame, imprisoned in the body. It is that life aspect which gives to man—as to

[4] *Webster's New International Dictionary*, Edition of 1923.
[5] *Ibid.*
[6] Radhakrishnan, S., *Indian Philosophy*, Vol. II, pp. 279, 283, 285.

all forms in manifestation—life, or being and consciousness. It is the vital factor, that integrating coherent something which makes the human being (composite, yet unified, as he is) a thinking, feeling and aspiring entity. The intellect in man is that factor or quality of soul-awareness which enables him to orient himself to his environment during the stages in which his personality is under development, but which later, through proper meditation, enables him to orient himself towards the soul, as detached from the mechanism, and thus, therefore, towards a new state of awareness of being.

The relation of the soul to the Oversoul is that of the part towards the Whole, and it is this relation and its consequent recognitions, which develop into that sense of oneness with all beings and with the supreme Reality to which the mystics have always testified. Its relation to the human being is that of the conscious entity towards its medium of expression; of the one who thinks, towards the instrument of thought; of the one who registers feeling, towards the field of sensuous experience, and of the actor, towards the physical body—the sole means of contact with that particular field of activity, the world of physical life. This soul expresses itself through two forms of energy, that which we call the vital principle or fluid, the life aspect, and the energy of pure reason. These energies are focussed during life in the physical body. The life stream centres itself in the heart, utilizing the blood stream, the arteries and the veins, and animating every part of the organism; the other stream, of intellectual energy, centres itself in the brain, and utilizes the nervous apparatus as its medium of expression. In the heart, therefore, is the seat of the life-principle; in the head is the seat of the reasoning mind and of the spiritual consciousness, which latter is attained through a right use of the mind. Dr. C. Lloyd Morgan says in connection with this word, "soul:"

"In any case what is currently understood by 'the soul-theory' has its roots in dualism. And what some people mean when they speak of 'a psychology without a soul' is a psychology other than dualistic. . . . There is, however, a sense in which he may, under suitable definition, speak of the soul as distinctive of that level of mental development at which a *concept* of Spirit is within the field of reflective reference."[7]

Earlier in the same book he says that:

"Each of us *is* a life, a mind, and Spirit—an instance of life as one expression of world-plan, of mind as a different expression of that world-plan, of Spirit in so far as the Substance of that world-plan is revealed within us. The world-plan, through and through, from its lowest to its highest expression, is manifestation of God; in you and me—in each of us severally—God as Spirit is partially revealed."[8]

It is this revelation of Deity that is the goal of the mystical endeavor and the object of the dual activity of mind—God as life in Nature, God as love, sub-jectively, and as plan and as purpose, and it is this that the unification, which meditation brings about

[7] Morgan, C. Lloyd, *Life, Mind and Spirit*, p. 35.
[8] *Ibid.*, p. 32.

reveals to man. Through its ordered technique, man discovers that unity which is himself. Through it, he later discovers his relation to the universe; he finds that his physical body and his vital energies are part and parcel of Nature itself, which is, in fact, the outer garment of Deity; he finds that his ability to love and to feel makes him aware of the love that pulses at the heart of all creation; and he discovers that his mind can give him the key which unlocks for him the door of understanding and that he can enter into the purposes and the plans which guide the Mind of God Himself. In fact, he arrives at God and discovers God as the central Fact. Knowing himself to be divine, he finds the whole is equally divine. Dr. F. Kirtley Mather of Harvard University has said in a most illuminating article:

"That there is an administration of the Universe cannot be denied. Something has determined and continues to determine the functioning of natural law, the orderly transformation of matter and of energy. It may be the 'curvature of the cosmos', or 'blind chance', or 'universal energy', or 'an absentee Jehovah', or an 'all-pervading Spirit', but it must be something. From one point of view, the question: Is there a God? is promptly answered in the affirmative."

Thus, through finding himself and understanding his own nature, man arrives at that centre within himself which is one with all that is; he finds he is equipped with an apparatus which can put him in touch with the differentiated manifestations through which Deity seeks to express itself. He possesses a vital body, responsive to universal energy, and the vehicle for the two forms of soul energy to which I referred above. The subject of the vital body, its relation to this universal energy, and its seven points of contact with the physical organism are covered in my book, *The Soul and Its Mechanism,* and will not be enlarged upon here, beyond quoting one paragraph.

"Behind the objective body lies a subjective form constituted of etheric matter, and acting as a conductor of the life principle of energy, or prana. This life principle is the force aspect of the soul, and through the medium of the etheric body the soul animates the form, gives it its peculiar qualities and attributes, impresses upon it its desires and, eventually, directs it through the activity of the mind. Through the medium of the brain the soul galvanizes the body into conscious (directed) activity and through the medium of the heart all parts of the body are pervaded by life."[9]

There is also another "body" which is composed of the sum-total of all emotional states, moods and feelings. This body reacts to a man's physical environment in response to information received by the brain through the medium of the five senses, and conveyed to it via the vital body. Thus it is swept into activity of a purely selfish and personal nature; or it can be trained to react primarily to the mind, regarding the mind (as it so seldom is) as the interpreter of the spiritual self, the soul. It is this emotional body, characterized by feeling and desire, that acts most potently, in the majority of cases, upon

[9] Bailey, Alice A., *The Soul and Its Mechanism,* p. 62.

the physical body. This latter is regarded by the esotericist as a pure automaton, driven into action by the desire nature and energized by the vital energy.

As the race progresses, another "body," the mind body, comes into being and activity, and gradually assumes an active and natural control. Like the physical and emotional organisms, this mental mechanism is at first entirely objective in its orientation, and swings into activity through impacts coming to it from the outer world, via the senses. Becoming increasingly positive, it slowly and surely begins to dominate the other phenomenal aspects of man until the personality, in all its four aspects, is completed and unified as a functioning entity on the physical plane. When this happens, a crisis is reached and new developments and unfoldments become possible.

All this time, the two energies of the soul, life and mind, have been working through the vehicles, without the man being aware of their source or purpose. As a result of their work, he is now an intelligent, active, high-grade human being. But, as Browning puts it: "In completed man begins anew a tendency to God,"[10] and he is driven by a divine unrest towards a conscious awareness of, and a conscious contact with, his soul—the unseen factor which he senses, but of which he remains personally unaware. Now he enters upon a process of self-education and of an intensive investigation into his true nature.

[10] Browning, Robert, *Paracelsus*.

His personality, which has been outgoing towards the world of physical, emotional and mental life, with its attention focussed objectively, goes through a process of reorientation, and turns inward towards the Self. Its focus becomes subjective and has for its purpose the emergence into manifestation of that "Deeper Being" about which Keyserling speaks. Conscious union with the soul is sought, and this not only from the emotional and sensuous angle of the devotee and mystic. Direct experience is sought. Knowledge of the divine Self, and mental assurance as to the fact of the indwelling Son of God becomes the goal of all endeavor. This method is not that of the mystical devotee who through the driving love of his emotional nature has sought after God. It is the method of intellectual approach and of the subordination of the entire personality to the drive towards spiritual realities. All purely mental types and all truly coordinated personalities are mystics at heart, and have passed through the mystical stage at some time or other *in some life*. As the intellect takes hold and the mind develops, this may temporarily fade into the background and be relegated for a time to the realm of the subconscious. But the emphasis is eventually and inevitably laid upon the will to know, and the drive of the life (no longer satisfied with the outer and external aspects of manifestation) is towards knowledge of the soul and the use of the mind in the apprehension of spiritual truth.

The head and the heart become united in their endeavor. Mind and pure reason are blended with

love and devotion in an entire re-adjustment of the
personality to a new realm of awareness. New states
of consciousness are registered, a new phenomenal
world is gradually perceived, and it begins to dawn
upon the aspirant that his life-focus and his consciousness can be lifted entirely out of all past fields
of endeavor. He finds that he can walk with God,
dwell in Heaven, and be aware of a new world lying
within the familiar outer forms. He begins to regard
himself as a conscious denizen of another kingdom in
nature, the spiritual, which is as real and as vital, as
ordered and as phenomenal as any we now know. He
steadily assumes the attitude of the soul towards his
instrument, the human body. He regards himself no
longer as a man, controlled by his emotions, impelled
by energy, and directed by his mind, but knows himself to be the Self, thinking through the mind, feeling
through the emotions, and acting consciously. As
this consciousness stabilizes and becomes permanent,
the work of evolution in his case is consummated,
the great at-one-ment is made, and the union between the Self and its vehicle of expression is established. Thus a divine Son of God consciously
incarnates.

Through the work of education in all its many
branches, the co-ordination of the personality has
been tremendously hastened. The mentality of the
race is steadily mounting the ladder of achievement.
Humanity, through its vast groups of educated and
mentally focussed people is ready for self-determination and soul-direction. Now the intensive cul-

ture of the individual, as taught in the Eastern system, can be undertaken. The education and re-orientation of the advanced human being must find its place in our mass education. This is the plea of this book and the object of its writing. How can a man find his soul, or ascertain the fact of its exist-ence? How can he re-adjust himself to the conditions of soul life, and begin to function consciously and simultaneously as a soul and as a man? What must he do to bring about that union between the soul and its instrument which is essential if the driving urge of his nature is ever to be satisfied? How can he know, and not just believe and hope and aspire?

The experienced voice of the eastern wisdom comes to us with one word:—Meditation. The ques-tion naturally arises: "Is that all?" and the answer is: "Yes." If meditation is rightly followed, and if perseverance is the keynote of the life, then increas-ingly soul contact is established. The results of that contact work out in self-discipline, in purification, and in the life of aspiration and of service. Medita-tion in the eastern sense is, as we shall see, a strictly mental process, leading to soul knowledge and il-lumination. It is a fact in nature that "as a man thinketh so is he."

Chapter Four

THE OBJECTIVES IN MEDITATION

"Union is achieved through the subjugation of the psychic nature, and the restraint of the mind-stuff. When this has been accomplished, the Yogi knows himself as he is in reality."

PATANJALI

The Objectives in Meditation

Assuming the correctness of the theories outlined in the preceding chapters, it might be of value if we were to state clearly toward what definite goal the educated man aims as he enters on the way of meditation, and in what way meditation differs from what the Christian calls prayer. Clear thinking on both these points is essential if we want to make practical progress, for the task ahead of the investigator is an arduous one; he will need more than a passing enthusiasm and a temporary endeavor if he is to master this science and become proficient in its technique. Let us consider the last point first, and contrast the two methods of prayer and of meditation. Prayer can perhaps be best expressed by certain lines, by J. Montgomery, well known to all of us.

> Prayer is the soul's sincere desire
> Uttered or unexpressed,
> The motion of a hidden fire,
> That trembles in the breast.

The thought held is that of desire, and of request; and the source of the desire is the heart. But it must be borne in mind that the heart's desire may be either for the acquisition of those possessions which the personality desires, or for those heavenly and transcendental possessions which the soul craves. Whichever it may be, the basic idea is demanding what is wanted, and the anticipation factor enters in; also something is eventually acquired, should the faith of the petitioner be sufficiently strong.

Meditation differs from prayer in that it is primarily an orientation of the mind, which orientation brings about realizations and recognitions which become formulated knowledge. Much confusion exists in the minds of many on this distinction and Bianco of Siena was really speaking of meditation when he said: "What is prayer but upward turning of the mind to God direct."

The masses of the people, polarized in their desire nature, and being predominantly of a mystical tendency, ask for what they need; they wrestle in prayer for the acquiring of longed-for virtues; they beg a listening Deity to assuage their troubles; they intercede for those near and dear to them; they importune high Heaven for those possessions—material or spiritual—which they feel essential to their happiness. They aspire and long for qualities, for circumstances and for those conditioning factors which will make their lives easier, or release them for what they believe will be freedom to be of greater usefulness; they agonize in prayer for relief from illness and disease, and seek to make God answer their request for revelation. But it is asking, demanding and expecting which are the main characteristics of prayer, with desire dominant, and the heart involved. It is the emotional nature and the feeling part of man which seeks after that which is needed, and the range of needs is wide and real. It is the heart approach.

Four degrees of prayer might be recognized:

1. Prayer for material benefits, and for help.
2. Prayer for virtues and for graces of character.
3. Prayer for others, intercessory prayer.
4. Prayer for illumination and for divine realization.

It will be seen from a study of these four types of prayer that all have their roots in the desire nature, and that the fourth brings the aspirant to the point where prayer can end and meditation begin. Seneca must have realized this when he said: "No prayer is needed, except to ask for a good state of mind, for health (wholeness) of soul."

Meditation carries the work forward into the mental realm; desire gives place to the practical work of preparation for divine knowledge and the man who started his long career and life experience with desire as the basic quality and who reached the stage of adoration of the dimly seen divine Reality, passes now out of the mystical world into that of the intellect, of reason, and eventual realization. Prayer, plus disciplined unselfishness, produces the Mystic. Meditation, plus organized disciplined service, produces the Knower. The mystic, as we have earlier seen, senses divine realities, contacts (from the heights of his aspiration) the mystical vision,

and longs ceaselessly for the constant repetition of
the ecstatic state to which his prayer, adoration and
worship have raised him. He is usually quite unable
to repeat this initiation at will. Père Poulain in *Des
Grâces d'Oraison* holds that no state is mystical unless the seer is unable to produce it himself. In
meditation, the reverse is the case, and through
knowledge and understanding, the illuminated man
is able to enter at will into the kingdom of the soul,
and to participate intelligently in its life and states
of consciousness. One method involves the emotional
nature and is based on belief in a God who can give.
The other involves the mental nature and is based
on belief in the divinity of man himself, though it
does not negate the mystical premises of the other
group.

It will be found, however, that the words mystic
and mystical are very loosely used and cover not
only the pure mystic, with his visions and sensory
reactions, but also those who are transiting into the
realm of pure knowledge and of certainty. They
cover those states which are unexpected and intangible, being based on pure aspiration and devotion, and also those which are the outcome of an ordered intelligent approach to Reality, and which are
susceptible of repetition under the laws which the
knower has learnt. Bertrand Russell deals with
these two groups in a most interesting way, though
he uses the one term Mystic in both relations. His
words form a most fascinating prelude to our theme.

"Mystical philosophy, in all ages and in all parts of the world, is characterized by certain beliefs which are illustrated by the doctrines we have been considering.

"There is, first, the belief in insight as against discursive analytic knowledge; the belief in a way of wisdom, sudden, penetrating, coercive, which is contrasted with the slow and fallible study of outward appearance by a science relying wholly upon the senses. . . .

"The mystic insight begins with the sense of a mystery unveiled, of a hidden wisdom now suddenly become certain beyond the possibility of a doubt. The sense of certainty and revelation comes earlier than any definite belief. The definite beliefs at which mystics arrive are the result of reflection upon the inarticulate experience gained in the moment of insight. . . .

"The first and most direct outcome of the moment of illumination is belief in the possibility of a way of knowledge which may be called revelation or insight or intuition, as contrasted with sense, reason and analysis, which are regarded as blind guides leading to the morass of illusion. Closely connected with this belief is the conception of a Reality behind the world of appearance and utterly different from it. This Reality is regarded with an admiration often amounting to worship; it is felt to be always and everywhere close at hand, thinly veiled by the shows of sense, ready, for the receptive mind, to shine in its glory even through the apparent folly and wickedness of Man. The poet, the artist, and the lover are seekers after that glory: the haunting beauty that they pursue is the faint reflection of its sun. But the mystic lives in the full light of the vision: what others dimly seek he knows, with a knowledge beside which all other knowledge is ignorance.

"The second characteristic of mysticism is its belief in unity, and its refusal to admit opposition or division anywhere. . . .

"A third mark of almost all mystical metaphysics is the

denial of the reality of Time. This is an outcome of the denial of division; if all is one, the distinction of past and future must be illusory. . . .

"The last of the doctrines of mysticism which we have to consider is its belief that all evil is mere appearance, an illusion produced by the divisions and oppositions of the analytic intellect. Mysticism does not maintain that such things as cruelty, for example, are good, but it denies that they are real: they belong to that lower world of phantoms from which we are to be liberated by the insight of the vision. . . ."[1]

But the mystical way is a preparation for the way of knowledge and where the mystic stops in adoration of the vision and in yearning after the Beloved, the seeker after true knowledge takes up the task and carries the work forward. Dr. Bennett of Yale says, at the close of his book on Mysticism, "The mystic at the end of his preparation is simply waiting for an apparition and an event which he is careful not to define too particularly; he is waiting, too, with the full consciousness that his own effort has now carried him as far as it can go and that it needs to be completed by some touch from without."[2] This thought confines the whole idea within the realm of sensuous perception, but there is something more. There is direct knowledge. There is an understanding of the laws governing this new realm of being. There is submission to a new procedure and to those steps and passwords which lead to the door and procure its opening. It is here that meditation plays its part

[1] Russell, Bertrand, *Mysticism and Logic*, pp. 8, 9, 10, 11.
[2] Bennett, Charles A., *A Philosophical Study of Mysticism*, p. 192.

and the mind steps in to fulfil its new function of revelation. Through meditation, the union for which the mystic yearns, and which he senses, and of which he has brief and fleeting experience, becomes definite and is known past all controversy, being recoverable at will. Father Joseph Maréchal in his notable book points out that:

". . . the symbol vanishes, imagery fades, space disappears, multiplicity is reduced, reasoning is silent, the feeling of extension gathers itself together and then breaks down; *intellectual activity is entirely concentrated in its intensity;* it seizes without intermediary, with the sovereign certitude of intuition, Being, God. . . .

"The human mind, then, is a *faculty in quest of its intuition*—that is to say of assimilation of Being, Being pure and simple, sovereignly *one*, without restriction, without distinction of essence and existence, of possible and real." [3] (Italics by A. A. B.)

To take the mind and bend it to its new task as a revealer of the divine is now the objective of the convinced mystic. To do this with success and with happiness, he will need a clear vision of his goal and a lucid understanding of the results eventually to be demonstrated. He will need a keen formulation of the assets with which he approaches his endeavor, and an equally keen appreciation of his lacks and defects. A view, as balanced as may be, of himself and of his circumstances, should be gained. Paralleling this, however, there should be also an equally balanced view of the goal and an understanding of

[3] Maréchal, Joseph, S.J., *Studies in the Psychology of the Mystics*, pp. 32, 101.

the wonder of the realizations and gifts which will be his, when his interest has been transferred from the things that now engross his attention, and his emotions, to the more esoteric values and standards.

We have touched upon the point that meditation is a process whereby the mind is reoriented to Reality, and, rightly used, can lead a man into another kingdom in nature, into another state of consciousness and Being and into another dimension. The goal of achievement has shifted into higher realms of thought and realization. What are the definite results of this reorientation?

It might be stated first of all that meditation is the science which enables us to arrive at direct experience of God. That in which we live and move and have our being is no longer the object of aspiration, or a symbol to us of a divine possibility. We know God as the Eternal Cause and the source of all that is, including ourselves. We recognize the Whole. We become one with God by becoming one with our own immortal soul, and when that tremendous event takes place we find that the consciousness of the individual soul is the consciousness of the whole, and that separativeness and division, distinctions and the concepts of me and thee, of God and a child of God, have faded away in the knowledge and realization of unity. Dualism has given place to unity. This is the Way of Union. The integrated Personality has been transcended through an ordered process of soul unfoldment, and a conscious at-one-ment has been brought about between the lower or personal self and the higher or divine self. This duality has to be first realized and then transcended before the Real Self becomes, in the consciousness of the man, the Supreme Self. It has been said that the two parts of man have had for long ages nothing in common; these two parts are the spiritual soul and the form nature, but they are joined eternally (and here lies the solution of man's problem) by the mind principle. In an ancient book of the Hindus, *The Bhagavad Gita*, these significant words are found:

"Self is the friend of self for him in whom the self is conquered by the Self; but to him who is far from the Self his own self is hostile like an enemy".[4]

and St. Paul says practically the same thing in his desperate cry:

"For I know that in me (that is, in my flesh,) dwelleth no good thing; for to will is present with me; but how to perform that which is good I find not. . . . For I delight in the law of God after the inward man: But I see another law in my members, warring against the law of my mind and bringing me into captivity to the law of sin which is in my members. O wretched man that I am! Who shall deliver me (the real Self) from the body of this death?"[5]

This real Self is God—God the triumphant, God the Creator, God the Saviour of man. It is, in the words of St. Paul, "Christ in us, the hope of glory." This becomes a fact in our consciousness and not simply a much hoped for theory.

[4] *Bhagavad Gita*, VI, 6.
[5] *Romans*, VII, 18, 22, 23, 24.

Meditation causes our beliefs to change into ascertained facts, and our theories into proven experience. The statement of St. Paul's remains only a concept and a possibility until, through meditation, the Christ life is evoked and becomes the dominating factor in daily life. We speak of ourselves as divine and as sons of God. We know of those who have demonstrated their divinity to the world, and who stand in the forefront of human achievement, testifying to faculties beyond our scope of accomplishment. We are conscious, within ourselves, of strivings which drive us on towards knowledge, and of interior promptings, which have forced humanity up the ladder of evolution to its present status of what we call educated human beings. A divine urge has driven us forward from the stage of the cave-dweller to our modern civilized condition. Above all, we are aware of those who possess, or claim to possess, a vision of heavenly things which we long to share, and who testify to a direct way into the centre of divine Reality which they ask us also to follow. We are told that it is possible to have direct experience, and the keynote of our modern times can be summed up in the words "From authority to experience." How can we know? How have this direct experience, free from the intrusion of any intermediary? The answer comes that there is a method which has been followed by countless thousands and a scientific process which has been formulated and followed by thinkers of all periods, and by means of which they become knowers.

The educational process has perhaps done its main work in preparing the mind to undertake the work of meditation. It has taught us that we possess such an apparatus and has presented to us some of its ways of use. The psychologists have told us much about our mental reactions, and our instinctual habits. Now man must possess himself consciously of his instrument and pass out of the initial stages of the educational process into that classroom and interior laboratory where it is possible to ascertain God for himself as the objective of all education. Who was it said that the world is not a prison house but a spiritual kindergarten, where millions of bewildered children are trying to spell God? The mind sends us hither and thither in the work of spelling out truth until the day dawns when, exhausted, we retire within ourselves and meditate and then find God. As Dr. Overstreet says: "All our enduring quest then gets its explanation and its significance. It is the God operative within ourselves. As, then, we discover the more enduring values, or as we create them, we enact God in our own lives."[6]

Again, we might define meditation as the method whereby a man reaches the glory of the unveiled self by the process of rejecting form after form. Education is not only purveyed in our schools and universities. The greatest school of all is life experience itself, and the lessons we learn are those we bring upon ourselves by identifying ourselves with a succession of forms—forms of pleasure, forms of those

[6] Overstreet, H. A., *The Enduring Quest*, p. 265.

we love, forms of desire, forms of knowledge—the list is endless! For what are forms but those substitutes which we create and then set in front of ourselves as objects of worship, or those ideas about happiness and truth which others have created and after which we endlessly run, only to find them fade away into mist before our tired eyes. We seek satisfaction in phenomena of all kinds, only to find them turn to dust and ashes, until we reach that something—intangible yet infinitely real—which gave being to them all. He who sees all forms as symbols of reality is well on the way to touching the unveiled Self. But it takes a mental apprehension and a guided intuition to do this. Did Sir James Jeans have a glimpse of this when he said:

"Phenomena come to us disguised in their frameworks of time and space; they are messages in cipher of which we shall not understand the ultimate significance until we have discovered how to decode them out of their space-time wrappings."[7]

Man is a point of divine light, hidden within a number of enveloping sheaths, as a light is hidden within a lantern. This lantern may be either closed and dark, or open and radiant. It may be either a light shining before men's eyes, or a hidden thing and, therefore, of no use to others. We are assured in that basic text book on meditation, the *Yoga Sutras of Patanjali*, of which an English paraphrase and commentary is furnished in my book *The Light of the Soul*, that through right discipline and medi-

[7] Jeans, Sir James, *The Universe Around Us*, p. 339.

tation "that which obscures the light is gradually removed," and that "when the spiritual intelligence . . . reflects itself in the mind-stuff then comes awareness of the Self.'"[8] At one point in the history of every human being there comes a momentous crisis when the light must be sensed, through a rightly used intelligence, and the Divine inevitably contacted. This Patanjali emphasizes when he says: "The transfer of the consciousness from a lower vehicle into a higher is part of the creative and evolutionary process.'"[9] Slowly and gradually the work of direct knowledge becomes possible, and the glory which is hidden behind every form can stand revealed. The secret is to know when that time has come and to seize the moment of opportunity. Meister Eckhart says:

"If the soul were stripped of all her sheaths, God would be discovered all naked to her view and would give himself to her, withholding nothing. As long as the soul has not thrown off all her veils, however thin, she is unable to see God."[10]

Thus, East and West teach the same idea and in the same symbology.

Meditation is, therefore, an ordered process whereby a man finds God. It is a system, well-tried out and much used, which unfailingly reveals the divine. The important words here are "ordered process." There are certain rules to be followed,

[8] Bailey, Alice A., *The Light of the Soul*, II., 52.
[9] *Ibid.*, IV., 2.
[10] Pfeiffer, Franz, *Meister Eckhart*, p. 114.

certain definite steps to be taken, and certain stages
of unfoldment to be experienced before a man can
garner the fruits of meditation. It is a part of the
evolutionary process, as we have seen, and like all
else in nature it is slow but sure, and unfailing in its
results. There is no disappointment to the man who
is willing to obey the rules and work with the system.
Meditation calls for self-control in all things, and
unless the work of meditating is itself accompanied
by the other requirements under the "ordered process" (such as self-control and active service) it will
fail in its objective. Fanaticism is not required. This
is made clear in the *Bhagavad Gita*:

"There is no meditation for the man who eats too little
or for the man who eats too much, or for him whose habit
it is to sleep too much or too little. But for him who is
regulated in food, in work; regulated also in sleep and in
waking, meditation becomes the destroyer of all suffering."[11]

Meditation can be regarded rightly as part of the
natural process which thus far has carried man forward along the path of evolution from a stage but
little removed from the animal to his present position of mental attainment, scientific achievement and
divine unrest. Steadily his centre of consciousness
has shifted, and steadily his attention has been
focussed on an ever widening range of contacts. Man
has already passed from the purely animal and
physical state of being into that of an intensely emotional and sensory awareness and in this state mil-

[11] *Bhagavad Gita*, VI., 16-17.

lions remain at this time. But other millions are progressing beyond this into another and higher field of awareness which we call that of the mind. Still another group, much fewer in number, are passing into a sphere where a universal range of contacts becomes possible. These we call the Knowers of the race. Through all methods employed runs the golden thread of divine purpose, and the way by which the transfer of the human consciousness into that of soul realization and soul awareness is effected is that of meditation.

This process of unveiling the Self through the negation of the form-side of life and the eventual inability of the various sheaths to hide it, can be described in terms of transmutation as well as in those of transference of consciousness.

Transmutation is the changing, and re-directing of the energies of the mind, of the emotions and of the physical nature so that they serve to reveal the Self, and not simply to reveal the psychical and body natures.

We are told, for instance, that we have five main instincts, which we share in common with all animals. These, when used with selfish and personal objectives, enhance the body life, strengthen the form or material nature and so serve increasingly to hide the Self, the spiritual man. These must be transmuted into their higher counterparts, for every animal characteristic has its spiritual prototype. The instinct of self-preservation must eventually be superseded by realization of immortality, and "dwelling ever in the Eternal," man will walk the earth and fulfill his destiny. The instinct which causes the lower self to thrust itself forward, and force its way upward, will eventually be transformed into the domination of the higher or spiritual Self. The assertion of the little or lower self will give way to that of the higher Self. Sex, which is an animal instinct powerfully governing all animal forms, will give place to a higher attraction, and will, in its noblest aspects, bring about conscious attraction and union between the soul and its vehicle; whilst the herd instinct will be transmuted into group consciousness. A fifth instinct, namely the urge to inquire and to investigate, which characterizes all minds at a high or a low level, will give place to intuitive perception and understanding, and so the great work will be accomplished and the spiritual man will dominate his creation, the human being, and lift all his attributes and aspects into heaven.

Through meditation, spiritual knowledge grows up within the mind, and from the basis of ordinary knowledge, we steadily expand our understanding of the term, until knowledge merges into wisdom. This is direct knowledge of God by means of the mental faculty, so that we become what we are, and are enabled to manifest our divine nature. Tagore, in one place, defines meditation as "the entering into some great truth until we are possessed by it," and truth and God are synonymous terms. The mind knows two objects, we are told—the outer world through the medium of the five senses and the brain, and the soul

and its world through what we might call an introverted use of the mind and its intense focussing upon
a new and unusual field of contact. Then "the mind-
stuff reflecting both the knower (the Self) and the
knowable, becomes omniscient . . . it becomes the
instrument of the Self and acts as a unifying
agent."[12] All things will stand revealed to the man
who truly meditates. He will comprehend the hidden
things of nature, and the secrets of the life of the
spirit. He will also know *how* he knows.

Thus, meditation brings about union, or at-one-
ment.

The Occidental mystic may speak of the At-one-
ment, whilst his brother in the Orient may speak of
Raja Yoga, or of Union and of liberation, but they
mean the same thing. They mean that the mind
and the soul (the Christ within us or the Higher
Self) function as a unit, as a co-ordinated whole,
thus expressing perfectly the will of the indwelling
God. René Guénon, in his book *Man and His Becoming*, makes the following interesting comments on the
word "union," which have a place here.

"The realization of this identity is effected by *Yoga*, that
is, the intimate and essential union of being with the Divine
Principle, or, if preferred, with the Universal. The proper
meaning of this word *Yoga* is in fact 'union' and nothing
else. . . . It should be noted that this realization ought not
strictly to be regarded as an 'achievement,' or as 'the production of a non-pre-existent result,' according to Shankarâchârya's expression, for the union in question, although not actually realized in the sense in which we here

[12] Bailey, Alice A., *The Light of the Soul*, IV., 22-24.

intend it, exists none the less potentially, or rather virtually; what is involved is merely the effectual attainment by the individual being . . . of the consciousness of that which truly is from all eternity.''[13]

Through the ordered stages of the meditation process, a relationship is gradually and steadily established between the soul and its instruments until the time comes when they are literally one. Then the sheaths serve simply to reveal the light of the indwelling Son of God; the physical body is under direct control of the soul, for the illuminated mind transmits (as we shall see later) soul knowledge to the physical brain; the emotional nature is purified and simply reflects the love nature of the soul, as the mind reflects the purposes of God. Thus, the hitherto disorganized and separative aspects of the human being are synthesized and unified and brought into harmonious relation with each other and with the soul, their creator, their source of energy, and their motivating power.

This science of union involves the disciplining of the life, and an experimental system of co-ordination. Its method is that of focussed attention, of mind control, or of meditation, and is a mode of development whereby we effect union with the soul, and become aware of inner states of consciousness. This is summed up for us in the familiar words of Browning:

> ''Truth is within ourselves; it takes no rise
> From outward things, whate'er you may believe.

[13] Guénon, René, *Man and His Becoming*, p. 37.

There is an inmost centre in us all,
Where truth abides in fulness; and around
Wall upon wall, the gross flesh hems it in,
    . . . and to know
Rather consists in opening out a way
Whence the imprisoned splendor may escape,
Than in effecting entry for a light
Supposed to be without.''[14]

The whole object of the science of meditation is, therefore, to enable man to become in outer manifestation what he is in inner reality, and to make him identify himself with his soul aspect and not simply his lower characteristics. It is a quick process for the unfolding of the reasoning consciousness, but in this instance must be self-applied and self-initiated. Through meditation, the mind is used as an instrument for observing the eternal states, and becomes in time an instrument for illumination, and through it the soul or Self transmits knowledge to the physical brain.

Finally, meditation brings about illumination. Meister Eckhart in his book of Sermons, written in the fourteenth century, says:

"Three kinds of men see God. The first see him in faith; they know no more of Him than they can make out through a partition. The second behold God in the light of grace but only as the answer to their longings, as giving them sweetness, devotion, inwardness and other such-like things. . . . The third kind see him in the divine light.''[15]

[14] Browning, Robert, *Paracelsus.*
[15] Pfeiffer, Franz, *Meister Eckhart*, p. 191.

It is this light that the process of meditation reveals and with which we learn to work.

The heart of the world is light and in that light shall we see God. In that light we find ourselves. In that light all things are revealed. Patanjali tells us that "when the means to union have been steadily practised and when impurity has been overcome, enlightenment takes place, leading up to full illumination." "The mind then tends towards increasing illumination as to the true nature of the Self."[16]

As a result of meditation comes the shining forth of the light. This "illumination is gradual and is developed stage by stage."[17]

This we shall take up in greater detail later on.

Through meditation, as a consequence of all the preceding factors, the powers of the soul are unfolded. Each vehicle through which the soul expresses itself carries latent within itself certain inherent potencies, but the soul, which is the source of them all, has them in their purest and most sublimated form. The physical eye, for instance, is the organ of physical vision. Clairvoyance is the same potency demonstrating in what is regarded as the psychical world—the world of illusion, of feeling and of emotion. But in the soul, this same power shows forth as pure perception, and infallible spiritual vision. The higher correspondences of the lower physical and psychical powers are brought

[16] Bailey, Alice A., *The Light of the Soul*, II., 27-28, IV., 26.
[17] *Ibid.*, III., 5-6.

into functioning activity through meditation, and so supersede their lower expressions.

These powers unfold normally and naturally. This they do, not because they are desired and consciously developed, but because as the inner God assumes control and dominates His bodies, His powers become apparent upon the physical plane and potentialities will then demonstrate forth as known realities.

The true mystic does not concern himself with the powers and faculties, but only with the Possessor of those powers. He concentrates upon the Self, and not upon the potencies of that Self. As he merges himself more and more in the Reality who is himself, the powers of the soul will begin to demonstrate normally, safely and usefully. The process is summed up for us by Meister Eckhart in these words:

"The soul's lower powers should be ordered to her higher and her higher ones to God; her outward senses to her inward, and her inward ones to reason; thought to intuition and intuition to the will and all to unity. . . ."[18]

The words of Dr. Charles Whitby, the translator of René Guénon's book, *Man and His Becoming,* are pertinent to this chapter on the objectives of the meditation process. He refers to the

". . . overwhelming testimony to the mutually-confirmatory agreement, on all essential points, of the Western, Hindu, Moslem and Far-Eastern esoteric traditions. The Truth we so rashly term unattainable awaits us there in

[18] Pfeiffer, Franz, *Meister Eckhart*, p. 40.

unchanged and changeless majesty, veiled indeed from hasty and scornful eyes, but ever increasingly apparent to earnest unbiased seekers. According to Plotinus, the act of contemplation which essentially constitutes the life of every individual and that of mankind as a whole, ascends gradually and by a natural and inevitable progression from Nature to Soul, from Soul to pure Intellect, from Intellect to the supreme 'One'. If this be so, the present pre-occupation with psychic or quasi-psychic matters of the more advanced representative of Western thought and science, may or rather must sooner or later be succeeded by an equally serious attention to matters of higher and even of highest import.''[19]

Thus it will be seen that the claims made for meditation are very high, and the weight of the testimony of the mystics and initiates of all the ages can be brought in corroboration of them. The fact that others have achieved may encourage and interest us but does no more unless we ourselves take some definite action. That there is a technique and a science of union, based on the right handling of the mental body and its correct use may be profoundly true, but this knowledge serves no purpose unless each educated thinker faces the issue. He must decide upon the values involved and set himself to demonstrate the fact of the mind, its relation in the two directions (to the soul on the one hand and to the outer environment on the other) and finally his ability to use that mind at will as he may choose. This involves the development of the mind as a synthesized, or common sense, and governs its use

[19] Guénon, René, *Man and His Becoming*, p. X.

in relation to the world of the earthly life, of the emotions and of thought. It involves also its orientation at will to the world of the soul, and its capacity to act as an intermediary between the soul and the physical brain. The first relation is developed and fostered through sound methods of exoteric education and of training; the second is made possible through meditation, a higher form of the educational process.

CHAPTER FIVE

STAGES IN MEDITATION

"What would you do within, O Soul, my Brother?
     What would you do within?
 Bar door and window that none may see:
     That alone we may be
          (Alone! face to face
          In that flame-lit place!)
     When first we begin
     To speak one with another."

                              EVELYN UNDERHILL

STAGES IN MEDITATION

WE HAVE studied briefly the objectives which we set before ourselves as we seek to reorient the mind to the soul, and through the union thus effected, enter into communication with a higher world of Being. We are seeking to utilize the equipment with which a long series of life experiments and experience has endowed us, and whether we undertake the work from the standpoint of the mystical devotee or the intellectual aspirant, there are certain basic requirements which must precede any definite exercises. The words of the Rev. R. J. Campbell state succinctly our story and our task. He says:

"For the purpose of realizing the nature of the Self, we have had to come out from our eternal home in God that we might strive and suffer amid the illusions of time and sense. We have to overcome before we can enter into the eternal truth that lies beyond all seeming. In that overcoming we have to master the flesh and magnify the spirit, despise the world to save it, and lose the life to find it."

Now let us consider the situation and the processes to which we must subject ourselves if the goal is ever to be attained. The preliminary requirements need only just be noted, for they are universally recognized and are met in part by every beginner, or he would not be entering upon this particular phase in the age-long pursuit of truth. We are conscious within ourselves of duality, and of a state of warfare between the two aspects of which we are constituted. We are conscious of a profound dissatisfaction with physical life as a whole, and with our inability to grasp and understand the divine Reality which we hope exists. But it remains for us a matter for faith, and we want certainty. The life of the senses does not seem to carry us far enough along the path towards our goal. It is a fluid existence which we lead, being sometimes carried by our high desires to a mountain top of wonder on which we stay just long enough to get a vision of beauty, and then are hurled into the abyss of our daily environment, our animal nature and the chaotic world in which our destiny places us. We sense a certainty which ever eludes us; we strive for a goal which seems outside ourselves and which evades our most frantic efforts; we struggle and fight and anguish to achieve a realization to which the saints have testified and to which the Knowers of the race bear continuous witness. If our will is strong enough and our determination rooted in steadfast and undeterred perseverance, and if the ancient rules and formulas are grasped, we can approach our problem from a new angle and utilize our mental equipment in place of emotional application and feverish desire.

The heart activity has its place, however, and Patanjali in his well known *Aphorisms*, which have guided the enterprise of hundreds of Knowers, says that:

"The practices which make for union with the soul are first, fiery aspiration, then spiritual reading and, lastly, complete obedience to the Master."[1]

The word "aspiration" comes from the Latin "*ad*"="to", and "*spirare*"="to breathe, to breathe towards," as Webster puts it. The word "spirit" comes from the same root. Aspiration must precede inspiration. There must be a breathing out from the lower self before there can be a breathing in by the higher aspect. From the standpoint of eastern mysticism, aspiration involves the idea of fire. It denotes a burning desire, and a fiery determination which eventually does three things for the aspirant. It throws a fierce light upon his problems, and constitutes the purificatory furnace into which the lower self has to go in order that all dross may be burned out, and it also destroys all hindrances which might keep him back. This same idea of fire runs through all books on Christian mysticism, and many passages in the Bible of a similar nature will come readily to mind. Willingness to "bear the cross," to "enter the fire," to "die daily," (it matters not what the symbology employed may be), is the characteristic of the true aspirant, and, before we pass on to the way of meditation and place our footsteps in those of the myriads of sons of God who have preceded us, we must gauge the depth and the

[1] Bailey, Alice A., *The Light of the Soul*, II., 1, 2.

height and brace ourselves for the arduous climb
and the fierce endeavor. We must say with J. C.
Earle:

> "I pass the vale. I breast the steep.
> I bear the cross: the cross bears me.
> Light leads me on to light. I weep
> For joy at what I hope to see
> When, scaled at length the arduous height,
> For every painful step I trod,
> I traverse worlds on worlds of light
> And pierce some deeper depth of God."[2]

We start with an emotional realization of our goal
and from then pass on, through the fire of discipline, to the heights of intellectual certainty. This
is beautifully pictured for us in the Bible in the story
of Shadrach, Meschach and Abednego. We read that
they were cast into the midst of the burning fiery
furnace, yet the result of that apparent tragedy was
the releasing in their midst of the form of a fourth
Identity, whose appearance was like unto that of
the Son of God. These three friends are symbols of
the threefold lower man. The name *Meschach* means
"agile," a faculty of the discriminative mind, the
mental body. *Shadrach* means "rejoicing in the
Way" and describes the transmutation of the emotional body, and the turning of the desire towards
the Way: *Abednego* means "a servant of the Sun,"
and thus emphasizes the fact that the sole function
of the physical body is to be the servant of the Son

[2] Earle, John Charles, *Onward and Upward* (Oxford Book of English Mystical Verse), p. 508.

(Sun), of the ego or soul (see Daniel III, 23-24). There is no escaping the fiery furnace, but the reward is commensurate with the trial.

The significance of the second requirement, spiritual reading, must also be grasped. The word, to "*read*," is very obscure in its origin, and philologists seem to think that two words are responsible. One is the Latin word "*reri*," to think, and the other the Sanskrit word "*radh*," to be successful. Perhaps both ideas are permissible, for it is certainly true that the man who can think the most successfully, and who can control and utilize his apparatus of thought, is the man who can the most easily master the technique of meditation.

Prayer is possible to all. Meditation is only possible to the mentally polarized man, and this is a point which needs emphasis and which frequently meets with opposition when stated. All men who are willing to subject themselves to discipline and transmute emotion into spiritual devotion can be saints, and many do so subject themselves. But *all men cannot yet be knowers*, for it involves all that the saint has achieved, plus the use of the intellect and the power to think through to knowledge and understanding. The man who is successful is the man who can think, and who can utilize the sixth sense, the mind, to produce certain specific results. Other suggested origins have to do with words denoting the taking of counsel or of advice, so that three basic ideas are brought out:—the attainment of success through the agency of the mind, the achievement of perfection, the taking of counsel, and the utilization of all channels of information in order to gain knowledge.

This is fundamentally the meaning of Patanjali when he uses the expression translated "spiritual reading." It really signifies reading with the eyes of the soul, with the inner vision alert to find out that which is sought. It is realized that all forms are only symbols of an inner or spiritual reality, and spiritual reading involves the development of the faculty of "reading" or seeing the life aspect which the outer form veils and hides. This will be found to apply equally to a human form as to any other form in nature; all forms veil a divine thought, idea, or truth and are the tangible manifestation of a divine concept. When a man knows this he begins to read spiritually, to see below the surface and so contact the idea which gave birth to the form. Gradually, as he gains practice in doing this, he arrives at a knowledge of Truth and is no longer taken in by the illusory aspects of the form. This, in its most practical application, will lead a man for instance, to negate the form aspect which his fellow-man may assume, and deal with him on the basis of the hidden divine reality. This is no easy thing to do, but it is possible through training in spiritual reading.

The third requirement is obedience to the Master. This is no servile attention to the commands of some supposed hidden Teacher, or Master, functioning mysteriously behind the scenes, as so many schools of esotericism claim. It is much simpler than that. The real Master, claiming our attention and subsequent obedience, is the Master in the Heart, the Soul, the indwelling Christ. This Master first makes His presence felt through the "still small voice" of conscience, prompting us to higher and more unselfish living, and sounding a quick note of warning when there is deviation from the strict path of rectitude. Later this comes to be known as the Voice of the Silence, that word that comes from the "Word incarnate," which is ourselves. Each of us is a Word made flesh. Later still, we call it the awakened intuition. The student of meditation learns to distinguish accurately between these three. This requirement, therefore, calls for that implicit obedience which the aspirant renders promptly to the highest impulse which he can register at all times and at any cost. When this obedience is forthcoming it calls forth from the soul a downpouring of light and knowledge, and Christ points this out in the words: "If any man shall do his will, he shall know . . ." (John 7, 17).

These three factors—obedience, a search for truth in every form, and a fiery longing for liberation— are the three parts of the stage of aspiration and must precede that of meditation. They need not be expressed in their fulness and completeness, but must be incorporated in the life as working rules of conduct. They lead to detachment, a quality which is emphasized both in the East and in the West. This is the freeing of the soul from the thralldom of the form life, and the subordination of the personality to the higher impulses. Dr. Maréchal expresses the Christian intention along these lines as follows:

"This 'detachment from self', what does it mean?

"First of all, clearly, it is detachment from the lower and sensible Ego—that is, the habitual subordination of the fleshly to the spiritual point of view, the co-ordination of the lower multiplicity under a higher unity.

"Again, it is detachment from the 'vainglorious Ego,' the dispersed and capricious Ego, the plaything of external circumstances, the slave of fluctuating opinion. The continuity of the inner life could not accommodate itself to so fluctuating a unity.

"Above all, it is detachment from the 'proud Ego.' We must have a right understanding of this, for humility is rightly considered as one of the most characteristic notes of Christian asceticism and mysticism."[3]

Here we have the subordination of the physical, emotional, and mental life to the divine project of achieving unity, emphasized, for capriciousness is a quality of the sensory apparatus, and pride that of the mind.

The meditation process is divided into five parts, one part leading sequentially to another. We will take these various stages and study each of them separately, for in their mastery we can trace the steady ascent of the conscious spiritual man out of the realm of feeling into that of knowledge and then of intuitive illumination. These stages might be briefly enumerated as follows:

[3] Maréchal, Joseph, S. J., *Studies in the Psychology of the Mystics*, p. 166.

1. *Concentration.* This is the act of concentrating the mind, learning to focus it and so use it.

2. *Meditation.* The prolonged focussing of the attention in any direction and the steady holding of the mind on any desired idea.

3. *Contemplation.* An activity of the soul, detached from the mind, which is held in a state of quiescence.

4. *Illumination.* This is the result of the three preceding processes, and involves the carrying down into the brain consciousness of the knowledge achieved.

5. *Inspiration.* The result of illumination, as it demonstrates in the life of service.

These five stages, when followed, lead to union with the soul and direct knowledge of divinity. For the majority of those who take up the study of meditation, the stage which should engross their attention for a long time—practically to the exclusion of the others—is that of concentration, the gaining control of the mental processes. Aspiration is presumably present to some degree or there would be no desire to meditate. It should be pointed out, however, that aspiration avails nothing unless it is endorsed by a strong will, a capacity to endure, and patient persistence.

I. *The Stage of Concentration.*

In all schools of advanced or intellectual mysticism, the first and necessary step is the attainment of mind control. Meister Eckhart, writing in the fourteenth century, tells us that!

"St. Paul reminds us that we being planted in the likeness of God may attain to higher and truer vision. For this

St. Dionysius says we require three things. The first is, possession of one's mind. The second is, a mind that is free. The third is, a mind that can see. How can we acquire this speculative mind? By a habit of mental concentration."[4]

This is in the strictest conformity with the eastern method, which aims first to put a man in control of his mental apparatus, so that he becomes the one who uses it at will and is not (as is so often the case) the victim of his mind, swayed by thoughts and ideas over which he has no control, and which he cannot eliminate, no matter how strong may be his desire to do so.

The same ideas that Meister Eckhart expressed can also be found in that ancient Indian Scripture, the *Bhagavad Gita*:

"The mind wavers, Krishna, turbulent, impetuous, forceful; I think it is as hard to hold as the wind.

"Without doubt . . . the wavering mind is hard to hold; but through assiduous practice . . . it may be held firm.

"When thy soul shall pass beyond the forest of delusion, thou shalt no more regard what shall be taught or what has been taught.

"When withdrawn from traditional teaching, thy soul shall stand steadfast, firm in soul vision, then thou shalt gain union with the soul."[5]

The first step, therefore, is mind control. This means the power to make the mind do as you want, to think as you choose, to formulate ideas and sequences of thought under direction. The function of

[4] Pfeiffer, Franz, *Meister Eckhart*, pp. 196-197.

[5] *Bhagavad Gita*, VI., 34-35, II., 52-53.

the mind, in the majority of cases, is first of all to receive messages from the outer world, via the five senses, and transmitted by the brain. Hume tells us that the "mind is a kind of theatre, where several perceptions successively make their appearance." It is the seat of the intellectual functions, and a great recording centre for impressions of all kinds, upon which we act, or to which we refuse admission if we do not like them. The mind has a tendency to accept what is presented to it. The ideas of the psychologists and of science as to the nature of the mind are too many to touch upon here. Some regard it as a separate entity; others as a mechanism, of which the brain and the nervous system are integral parts. One school deals with it as "a sort of superior, non-physical structure . . . capable of strict scientific study and liable to its own disorders." Some look upon it as a form of the self, with a life of its own; as a defense mechanism built up during the ages; as a response apparatus through which we contact aspects of the Universe otherwise untouchable. To some, it is simply a vague term signifying that by which we register thought or respond to vibrations, such as those incorporated in public opinion and in the books written throughout the ages. To the esotericist, it is simply a word standing for an aspect of man which is responsive in one direction—the outer world of thought and of affairs—but which could be equally responsive in another—the world of subtle energies and of spiritual being. This is the concept we shall hold in our thoughts as we study

the technique of meditation. Dr. Lloyd Morgan sums
it up for us in such a way that all lesser definitions
are included. He says:

". . . the word 'mind' may be used in three senses;
first, as Mind or Spirit in reference to some Activity, for
us God; secondly, as a quality emergent at a high level of
evolutionary advance; and thirdly, as a psychical attribute
that pervades all natural events in universal correlation."[6]

Here we have the idea of the divine purpose, the
universal mind, of that human mentality which distinguishes man on the ladder of evolution from the
animals, and reference also to that universal psychical consciousness which pervades the animate and
the so-called inanimate. It is with mind as a quality
emerging at a high level of evolution that we as
human beings deal. It is for us a mode or means of
contact, receiving information from various sources,
and by different means. Through the five senses, information is conveyed, and the man becomes aware
of the world of physical phenomena and of psychical
life in which he is immersed. Not only that, but the
mind registers impressions emanating from other
minds, and the thoughts of men (both ancient and
modern) are conveyed to him through the medium
of reading and the spoken word, through the drama,
through pictures and through music. Most of it is
simply registered and stored up, finding later expression as memory and anticipation. Moods, emotional reactions, feelings and desires, are also re-

[6] Morgan, C. Lloyd, *Emergent Evolution,* p. 37.

corded by the mind, whether of a high grade or a low, but with the average person that is all that happens. Very little real thinking follows upon the registering of information, and no clear formulation of thoughts occurs. The clothing of ideas with words which clearly express them is one of the functions of the mind, yet, how few people have ideas or originate really intelligent thoughts! Their minds respond to that which is conveyed to them from the outer world, but have no inherent or self-initiated activities of their own.

Therefore, the process at present controlling in the case of the average man is from the outside world inwards, through the senses, to the brain. The brain then "telegraphs" the information registered to the mind, which, in its turn, records it. That usually closes the incident.

But, in the case of the truly thoughtful, there is more than this. Upon the recording follows an analysis of the incident or the information, its correlation with other incidents, and a study of cause and effect. The "mind-stuff," as the Oriental calls it, is swept into activity, and thought-forms are created and mental images built in connection with the presented idea. Then, if desired, the clear thinking of the man is impressed upon the brain and so a return activity is instituted. But, in the case of the mystic and of the man who is beginning to meditate, something further is discovered. He finds that the mind, when properly governed and disciplined, is capable of wider and deeper responses; that it can become

aware of ideas and concepts which emanate from
a deeply spiritual realm and which are communicated by the soul. Instead of impressions from the
outer daily life recorded on the sensitive receiving-
plate of the mind, they may come forth from the
kingdoms of the soul and are caused by the activity
of a man's own soul, or by other souls with whom his
soul may be in touch.

Then the mind enters upon a new and fresh usefulness and its range of contact includes not only
the world of men but also the world of souls. Its
function is to act as an intermediary between the
soul and the brain and to transmit to the brain
that of which the man, as a soul, has become aware.
This becomes possible when the old mental activities are superseded by the higher, and when the
mind can be rendered temporarily insensitive to all
outer calls upon its attention. This, however, is not
brought about by any methods of rendering the mind
passive and receptive, or by any system of "blank-
ing" the mind, or stunning it into negativity, or
other forms of self-hypnotism. It is caused by the
expulsive force of a new and bigger interest, and by
the one-pointed attention of the focussed mental
faculties to a new world of phenomena and of force.
This system is that of concentration, the first and
most arduous step towards the illumination of the
life.

The word "concentration" comes from the Latin
words "con"="together" and "centrare"="to
centre." It means the "bringing together or the

drawing to a common centre or focal point;" it connotes the gathering together of our wandering thoughts and ideas, and holding the mind firmly and steadily focussed or centred on the object of our immediate attention, without wavering or distraction. It involves the elimination of all that is foreign or extraneous to the matter under observation. Patanjali defines it thus: "The binding of the perceiving consciousness to a certain region is attention or concentration."[7]

This necessarily involves a distinction between the Thinker, the apparatus of thought, and that which is to be considered by the Thinker. We need, therefore, to distinguish between ourselves, the one who is thinking and that which we use to think with, the mind. Then there comes in the third factor, that which is thought.

Students would do well at the very beginning of their meditation work to learn to make these basic differentiations, and to cultivate the habit every day of making these distinctions. They must distinguish always between:

1. The Thinker, the true Self, or the Soul.
2. The mind, or the apparatus which the Thinker seeks to use.
3. The process of thought, or the work of the Thinker as he impresses upon the mind (when in a state of equilibrium) that which he thinks.
4. The brain, which is in its turn impressed by the mind, acting as the agent for the Thinker, in order to convey impressions and information.

[7] Bailey, Alice A., *The Light of the Soul*, III., 1.

Concentration is, therefore, the power to focus the consciousness on a given subject and to hold it there as long as desired; it is the method of accurate perception, and the power to visualize correctly, being the quality which enables the Thinker to perceive and know the field of perception. Another word for concentration is attention, that is, one-pointed attention. It is interesting to note what Father Maréchal says in this connection. He points out that "attention is a *direct path* to full perception, to hallucination, or, more generally, to belief. . . . It brings about an at least momentary *unification* of the mind by the predominance of one mental group. . . . But this 'mental unity,' realized to some degree in the phenomenon of attention, is also the *sole subjective condition* which, we have seen, accompanies *always* the true or false perception of the real."[8]

The question may be asked, what is the easiest way to teach oneself to concentrate? One might reply, in the words of the French proverb: "Le meilleur moyen de déplacer est de remplacer;"—"the best way to eliminate is to substitute," and one way that may be employed is to utilize what has been called the "expulsive power of a new affection." To be profoundly interested in some new and intriguing subject, and to have one's attention focussed on some fresh and dynamic matter will automatically tend to make the mind one-pointed.

[8] Maréchal, Joseph, S. J., *Studies in the Psychology of the Mystics,* p. 90.

A second answer might be given: Be concentrated in all that you do all day every day. Concentration will be rapidly developed if we cultivate the habit of accuracy in all the affairs of life. Accurate speech would necessitate accurate attention to that which is said, read or heard, and this would necessarily involve concentration and so develop it. True meditation is after all an attitude of mind and will grow out of an attitude of concentration.

The objective, therefore, of all our endeavor is to train the mind so as to make it our servant and not our master, and to cultivate the power of concentration preparatory to true meditation work. The earnest student, therefore, will carry this close attention into the affairs of everyday life and will thereby learn to regulate his mind as an apparatus for his thought.

Let me emphasize here the necessity of a constantly concentrated attitude to life. The secret of success can be expressed in the simple words: Pay attention. In talking to people, in reading a book, in writing a letter, let us steadily focus our thought on what we are doing and so gradually develop the capacity to concentrate.

To this cultivated attitude there must be added definite concentration exercises, carried forward each day, with perseverance. This involves the fixing of the mind upon a particular object, or a chosen topic for thought. To this succeeds a process of steadily and quietly learning to abstract the consciousness from the outer world and exoteric conditions and focus it at will on any subject.

The regular unremitting work of daily concentration gradually overcomes the difficulty of control and brings about results which might be enumerated as follows:

1. The reorganization of the mind.
2. The polarizing of the man in his mental, instead of his emotional vehicle.
3. The withdrawal of the man's attention from the sense perceptions and his learning to centre himself in the brain. Most people, like the animals, use the solar plexus.
4. The development of a faculty of instantaneous concentration as a preliminary to meditation.
5. The capacity to focus the attention unswervingly upon any chosen seed thought.

II. *The Stage of Meditation.*

Patanjali defines concentration as the holding of the perceiving consciousness in a certain region and meditation as the prolonged holding of the perceiving consciousness in a certain region. This implies only a difference in the time factor and would seem to make of both stages an achievement of control. Through the practice of concentration sufficient control should be achieved, so that the student is not bothered by the necessity of repeatedly recollecting his thought. Therefore, an act of prolonged concentration gives opportunity for the mind to act upon whatever object lies within the ring-pass-not of the region chosen. The choosing of a word or a phrase as the subject of the meditation establishes this ring-pass-not and if the meditation is well conducted the mind never leaves its consideration of the object so chosen. The mind remains focussed and is continuously active during the entire meditation period. Moreover, the mind is not allowed to do as it pleases with the object, or seed thought. In concentration there should be a consciousness in the meditator all the time that he is using his mind. In meditation this consciousness of the mind being used is lost, but there can be no day-dreaming and no following of chance ideas which emerge in relation to the object of thought. The seed thought has been chosen for a purpose,—either for its effect on the meditator or for its effect in service upon some other person or in relation to some spiritual work, or in some phase of the search for wisdom. If the process is successful, there is evoked little or no reaction in the meditator, either of pleasure or absence of pleasure. Emotional reactions are transcended and the mind is, therefore, left free to act in its own right. The result is a clarity of thought never before achieved, because the mind in ordinary activity is always associated with and affected by desire of some sort. In this state of consciousness desire is transcended, just as later in the stage of contemplation, thought is transcended. When the mind is stunned into inaction by inhibition or persistent repetitions, it cannot be transcended in contemplation, nor used in meditation. To practise making the mind blank, is not only foolish, but actually dangerous.

In *The Yoga Sutras of Patanjali* we find these words:

"The gradual conquest of the mind's tendency to flit from one object to another and the power of one-pointedness make the development of contemplation."[9]

Meditation is the result of experience. It is the instantaneous attainment of an attitude of mind as a consequence of long practice. In the *Bhagavad Gita* we find it is stated that in all action the five following factors are involved:

"1. The material instrument .... the brain
2. The doer .... the Self
3. The organ .... the mind
4. The impulse .... energy
5. Destiny .... Karma"[10]

Meditation is activity of a very intense kind and it will be found that all these five factors are involved. The material instrument which we have to use in meditation is the physical brain. Many people think that they must transcend the brain, reach some tremendous altitude and stay upon some pinnacle of thought until something transcendent happens, and they can then say they know God. What is really needed is that we should get control of the mind and of the brain processes, so that the brain becomes a sensitive receiver of the thoughts and desires of the soul, the Higher Self, as He transmits them through the medium of the mind. The mind is regarded as in

[9] Bailey, Alice A., *The Light of the Soul*, III., 11.
[10] *Bhagavad Gita*, XVIII., 13-14.

the nature of a sixth sense, and the brain as a receiving plate. We are already utilizing the five senses as avenues of perception, and they telegraph constant information to the brain. Through their medium, information as to five vast fields of knowledge, or of five ranges of vibrations, is made available to man. It is intended that the mind should serve a similar purpose. This is summarized for us by Meister Eckhart, and embodies the position of all the mystics in both hemispheres:

"First, see that thy outward senses are properly controlled. . . . Now turn to the inward senses or noble powers of the soul, lower and higher. Take the lower powers first. These are intermediate between the higher powers and the outward senses. They are excited by the outward senses; what the eye sees, what the ear hears, they offer forthwith to desire. This offers it again, in the ordinary course, to the second power, called judgment, which considers it and once more passes it on to the third power, reckoning or reason. . . .

"A man, moreover, must have a mind at ease . . . the body should be rested from bodily labor, not only of the hands but of the tongue as well and all five senses. The soul keeps clear best in the quiet, but in jaded body is oft overpowered by inertia. Then by strenuous effort we travail in divine love for intellectual vision, till, clearing a way through recollected senses, we rise past our own mind to the wonderful wisdom of God. . . . Man rising to the summit of his mind is exalted God."[11]

Through the agency of the mind as a directed instrument, the soul can manipulate the impulses or thought currents. These forces pour into the field of

[11] Pfeiffer, Franz, *Meister Eckhart*, pp. 279, 47.

experience of the Thinker and he must learn to direct them consciously and to work with them, so as to produce the desired result.

The fifth factor reminds us that a certain stage of evolutionary development must be reached before true meditation becomes possible; certain work must be done and certain refinements in our instrument made, before a man can safely and wisely meditate. All men are not equipped to meditate with hope of complete success. This need in no way discourage any student. A beginning can always be made and a sound foundation laid. The control of the mental processes can be begun, and brought to a high point of achievement, making it possible for the soul to have an apparatus of thought ready to its use. Re-acting to the three parts of the meditation, but re-acting in a unified manner the physical or form nature has been studied, the quality animating it and the motive or cause of the manifestation of the form has been considered. At the same time there has been an ever deeper concentration, and a more intense meditation. The attention has sunk inward increasingly, and outer things have been steadily negated; this has not been accomplished through a passive attitude, but through one of a most keen and vital interest. The meditation has been positive in its method and has not led to a negative or trance condition. The mind has been busy all the time, but busy in one direction.

Finally, there comes the stage which is called

bliss, or identification. The consciousness is no longer focussed in the intellect but becomes identified with the object of the meditation work. This we will consider later.

We have, therefore, the four stages briefly summarized as follows and constituting what is called "meditation with seed:"

1. Meditation on the nature of a particular form.

2. Meditation upon the quality of a particular form.

3. Meditation upon the purpose of a particular form.

4. Meditation upon the life animating a particular form.

All forms are symbols of an indwelling life, and it is through meditation with seed that we arrive at the life aspect.

In *A Treatise on Cosmic Fire* the following words occur:

"The wise student regards all forms of expression as in the nature of symbols. A symbol has three interpretations; it is itself the expression of an idea, and that idea has behind it, in its turn, a purpose or impulse inconceivable as yet. The three interpretations of a symbol might be dealt with as follows:

"1. *The exoteric interpretation* of a symbol is based largely upon its objective utility, and upon the nature of the form. That which is exoteric and substantial serves two purposes:

"*a*. To give some faint indications as to the idea and concept. This links the symbol . . . with the mental plane, but does not release it from the three worlds of human appreciation.

"*b*. To limit and confine and imprison the idea and so adapt it to the point in evolution which the man has reached. The true nature of the latent idea is ever more potent and complete than the form or symbol through which it seeks expression. Matter is a symbol of a central energy. Forms of all kinds in all the kingdoms of nature, and the manifested sheaths in their widest connotation and totality are but symbols of life—what that Life itself may be remains as yet a mystery.

"2. *The subjective interpretation* or meaning is the one which reveals the idea lying behind the objective manifestation. This idea, incorporeal in itself, becomes a concretion on the plane of objectivity. . . . These ideas become apparent to the student after he has entered into Meditation, just as the exoteric form of the symbol is all that is seen by the man who is just beginning. As soon as a man begins consciously to use his mental apparatus and has made even a small contact with his soul three things occur:

"*a*. He reaches out beyond the form and seeks to account for it.

"*b*. He arrives in time at the soul which the

form veils, and this he does through the understanding of his own soul.

"*c*. He begins then to formulate ideas and to
create and make manifest that soul-energy or
substance which he finds he can manipulate.

"To train people to work in mental matter is
to train them to create; to teach people to know
the nature of the soul is to put them in conscious
touch with the subjective side of manifestation
and to put into their hands the power to work
with soul-energy; to enable people to unfold the
potencies of the soul aspect is to put them *en
rapport* with the forces and energies hidden in
all the kingdoms of Nature.

"A man can then—as his soul contact and his
subjective perception is strengthened and developed—become a conscious creator, co-operat-
ing with the plans of evolution and of God. As
he passes through the different stages, his ability so to work and his capacity to get at the
thought lying behind all symbols and forms in-
creases. He is no longer taken in by the appearance but knows it as the illusory form which is
veiling, imprisoning and confining some thought.

"3. *The spiritual meaning* is that which lies
behind the subjective sense and which is veiled
by the idea or thought just as the idea is veiled
by the form it assumes when in exoteric manifestation. This can be regarded as the purpose
which prompted the idea and led to its emana-
tion into the world of forms. It is the central

dynamic energy which is responsible for the subjective activity. . . .''[12]

It is this process of arriving at the reality behind each and every form which is the result of meditation with seed. It involves the realization of these three aspects of the divine Life. This is why students are advised to take some specific words or a verse from some sacred book for their meditation so as to train them in their power to get behind the form of the words and so to arrive at the true meaning.

We have penetrated into the world of causes; we have to seek to apprehend the Plan as it exists in the mind of God and as it expresses itself through the love, emanating from the Heart of God. Is it possible for human minds to reach any further than the love and will of God? Right at this point, Divinity is contacted. The mind ceases to function, and the true student of meditation slips into a state of conscious identification with that spiritual reality we call the indwelling Christ, the divine Soul. Man, at this point, enters into God.

[12] Bailey, Alice A., *A Treatise on Cosmic Fire*, pp. 1233 et seq.

CHAPTER SIX

STAGES IN MEDITATION (*Continued*)

Milarepa was one who eventually rid himself of the
Two-Fold Shadow and soared into Spiritual Space, till
he attained the Goal wherein all doctrines merge in
at-one-ment. . . . Having all his ideas and concepts
merged with the Primal Cause (he) had eliminated the
Illusion of Duality.

RECHUNG (from the Tibetan)

STAGES IN MEDITATION (*Continued*)

WE HAVE carried our meditation work forward along what might be termed secular lines, for the use of the mind has been involved, and though the subject of the meditation process has presumably been religious, yet the same results can be equally well reached with a purely worldly theme as the "object" or "seed thought." The educating of the mind to hold itself attentively upon a chosen idea has been the aim. We have, therefore, been dealing with what might legitimately be called a part of the educational process.

It is at this point that the divergence of our eastern and western methods becomes apparent. One school teaches its students to gain control of the instrument of thought before anything else is done, to discover the existence of this instrument through primary failure in control, and then, through concentration and meditation, to achieve facility in forcing the mind to be one-pointed in any direction. The other school posits the possession of something that is called the mind, and proceeds then to fill it with information, and to train the memory aspect to be retentive, and the content of that memory to be easily available to the student. From this stage a relatively few in number pass on to a real use of the mind through a profound interest in some science or some way of living, but the majority never attain mind control. Educational methods as we now have them do not teach their students this preliminary technique, and, hence, the wide confusion as to the nature of the mind and as to the distinction between the mind and the brain.

If the brain and the brain cells are all that there is, then the position of the materialistic thinker, that thought is entirely dependent upon the quality of the brain cells, is logical and correct. The part that the brain plays in the process is ably put for us in Ludwig Fischer's book, *The Structure of Thought*:

"The perfection of processes of apprehension depends in the main on the structure and functioning of a certain organ which receives and connects the different impressions of the senses, and which, further, partly retains the traces of previous impressions and allows them indirectly to enter into action. This organ is the brain with its ramifications and subsidiary organs. The perfection of the structure and of the functioning of this organ determines the perfection with which we can succeed in a deliberate attempt at producing a representation of the complex of the Whole, using the specific forms of sensual perception which are at our command. . . .

"The brain allows us to have an intuition and an intellectual apprehension of the world in its complexity. The manner in which this is brought about depends on the exceedingly complicated internal structure of this organ, and on its reciprocal relation to the other parts of the Whole, a relation which has many gradations."[1]

[1] Fischer, Ludwig, *The Structure of Thought*, p. 135.

If perception and sensuous apprehension, with their consequent rationalizings and the institution of a subsequent mental process, have their source in the brain, then Dr. Sellars is right in his book, *Evolutionary Naturalism*, when he says that mind can be regarded as a "physical category" and that "we should mean by it the nervous processes which find expression in intelligent conduct."[2]

But this idea fails to satisfy the majority of thinkers and most of them—belonging to other schools than the purely materialistic—posit something more than matter, and regard the mind as distinct from the brain; they hold the hypothesis that it is a subjective substantial reality, which can use the brain as its terminal of expression and which it can impress in order to express those concepts and intuitions which a man can consciously utilize. What we are considering is in no wise a supernormal faculty, or the possession of a specialized instrument by a gifted few; the mind should be used by all educated people, and at the close of the educational process (carried on in the formative years) a man should be in possession of a faculty that he understands and uses at will. Dr. McDougall points out in *Psychology, the Science of Behavior* that our mental activity (which is usually unconscious) can be either subnormal, normal or supernormal.[3] In the first case, you will have the idiot or the feeble-minded; in the second, you will have the intelligent average citizen

[2] Sellars, Dr. Roy Wood, *Evolutionary Naturalism*, p. 300.
[3] McDougall, William, *Psychology, the Science of Behavior*.

whose mind is a theatre or rather a cinematograph, registering anything that happens to come along; and, finally, we shall discover those rare souls whose consciousness is illuminated and whose minds record that which is hidden to the majority. With this last class we have as yet nothing to do. They are the product of the final stages of the meditation work,— contemplation and illumination. Concentration and meditation have definite reference to the many and to the normal.

In the East, and by many in the West, the mind is regarded as separate and distinct from the brain. Dr. C. Lloyd Morgan in *Emergent Evolution* quotes Descartes as saying that "there are indeed (1) corporeal substance (*res extensa*), and (2) mental or thinking substance (*res cogitans*); but they need for their being the concurrence of God. . . . Apart from this common dependence on God neither is dependent on the other."[4] He sums up his own point of view in another book, *Life, Mind, and Spirit*, as follows:

"Spirit is nowise separable from life and mind, nor they from it. What is given for reflective contemplation is a world-plan of natural events. I hold that this world-plan is a manifestation of Divine Purpose. . . . We too are manifestations of Spirit which is 'revealed' within us. Each of us *is* a life, a mind, and Spirit—an instance of life as one expression of the world-plan, of mind as a different expression of that world-plan, of Spirit in so far as the Substance of that world-plan is revealed within us. . . . This revelation is only partial since each of us is only an indi-

4 Morgan, C. Lloyd, *Emergent Evolution*, p. 291.

vidual instance of that which in full manifestation is universal.''[5]

God reveals His purpose through the activity of the form. He does the same through the activity of the mind, which impresses in its turn the brain, attuned to receptivity. Later again, the mind becomes responsive to an illumination, emanating from the Spirit aspect, and this we will shortly consider. This approaches very close to the Oriental position which infers a ''mind-stuff'' which is thrown into activity from the outer world of human affairs by the agency of the senses, by the emotions and by other minds. This intense activity of the mind-stuff has to be definitely offset through concentration and meditation if the mind is to be brought into a condition wherein it can be refocussed and reoriented to another field of perception and another range of ideas. For the esotericists, therefore, the objective of the meditation (carried forward into its later stages) is that the mind should cease to register any form activity whatsoever, no matter of how high an order, but should begin to register impressions emanating from that steadily manifesting Factor which we call (for lack of a better term) the Mind of God, the Universal Mind. This mind is distinguished by a sense of Wholeness, and of synthesis.

The entire history of evolving humanity might be considered from the angle of this Plan concept, and the focus of interest might be noted to be that of a growing consciousness in man of a Universe which

[5] Morgan, C. Lloyd, *Life, Mind, and Spirit*, p. 32.

is a revelation of a Life and of Deity, and in which mankind plays its part in the greater Whole. Ludwig Fischer calls our attention to the fact that all our faculties "are founded on the mysterious and unconscious something which dominates the whole of our intellectual life," and points out the necessity for what he calls the non-rational element in the answers which we give to the complex questions of every day. His conclusions as to the basic situation which man has to face in connection with thought and our progress into higher and non-rational realms are true and forceful. He says:

"One way of advancing only is possible. The way is led by the intuition of minds of a more than average instinctive sensitiveness; analytical reason follows, consolidating the position and making practicable the road for the rest of mankind. The advance into the unknown begins with a hypothesis, and a hypothesis is nothing but a more or less non-rational structure, obtained intuitively. Once it has been set up, it is compared in all its implications with experience, so that, if possible, the hypothesis can be tested and rationalized."[6]

We have reached the stage in our study of the process of mind control when we must proceed upon hypothesis. Yet, primarily, it will be hypothesis only to the materially-minded, for the conclusions reached and the realm of knowledge entered are recorded as truth and proven fact by many thousands down the ages.

We have outlined a method, old and tried, whereby it is claimed the mind can be grasped and used at

[6] Fischer, Ludwig, *The Structure of Thought*, p. 361.

will, and we have pointed out a way in which the factors which have hitherto engrossed its attention can be negated and a new field of awareness become possible. Before carrying the instructions forward, it might be of value if we defined the hypothesis upon which we will now proceed. It might be expressed as follows:

There is a kingdom of the soul, called often the kingdom of God, which is in reality another kingdom in nature, a fifth kingdom. Entry into that kingdom is as much a natural process as has been the transit of the evolving life from any kingdom in nature to another in the process of evolution. When the senses, and all that they convey, are focussed into that "common-sense," which was the name that mystics such as Meister Eckhart gave to the mind, they enrich that mind and open up to it many states of awareness. When these activities can be negated and the rich and sensitive mind can be refocussed in its turn, it becomes a sensitive apparatus (a sixth sense, if you like) which registers "the things of the kingdom of God" and opens up, to the man in deep meditation, states of consciousness and ranges of knowledge which have hitherto been sealed to him but which are just as much a part of the Whole and of the world content as any other field of investigation. This is our hypothesis and upon it we will proceed. Instinctual awareness has given place in man to intellectual knowledge. Is it not possible that this intellectual perception may, in its turn, be transcended and superseded by intuitional awareness?

Certain propositions seem necessary at this point in our argument and may be of value in elucidating the theme of this book: They are three in number.

First: In the long evolutionary process which has led man from the animal stage to that of the human being, we find that we have now arrived at the phase in which he is self conscious, or self-referring. He stands at the centre of his own world, and the universe revolves around him. All that occurs has reference to him and to his affairs, and to the effect of life and circumstance upon him as the important factor.

Second: As man grows in knowledge and in intellectual awareness, the brain and the mind become co-ordinated. The former becomes simply the tool or instrument of the trained instincts and of the controlled mind. This mind draws on what has been called "the content of the subconscious," on the active memory, and on the environment, for what is needed to carry forward the process of living in an exigent world. Man becomes an efficient and useful human being, and takes his place as a conscious cell in the body of humanity. He is beginning to get some realization of group relations. But more remains.

Third: From the earliest stage of human existence up to that of the high grade co-ordinated functioning man, there has always been present a consciousness of something Other, of a factor lying beyond known human experience, of a goal or quest, of a Deity. This subtle and indefinable awareness emerges inevitably and keeps man pushing forward, and seeking for that which neither the mind (as he knows it) nor his circumstances and environment seem able to give. This can be called the search for certainty, an endeavor after the mystic experience, or the religious impulse. But no matter by what name we call it, it is unfailingly present.

These three propositions roughly outline the way that man, in his consciousness, has travelled. They portray the condition in which we find a vast number of human beings at this time—efficient, intellectual, well-informed, responsible, but at the same time, dissatisfied. They look with questioning into the future or face the inevitability of death; they are anxious to go forward into a wider consciousness and into a certainty as to spiritual things and as to the ultimate Reality. This urge to a wider understanding and knowledge is being demonstrated on a large scale at this time, and the sequence of the evolutionary growth, already established, is apparently persisting and must do so if another kingdom or state of consciousness is to be added to those already achieved.

It is at this point that all the great world religions offer to man a way of knowledge and a process of unfoldment which can and does hasten the work of development. Dr. Otto in *The Idea of the Holy* says that man "must be guided and led on by consideration and discussion of the matter through the ways of his own mind, until he reach the point at which the 'numinous' in him perforce begins to stir, to start into life and into consciousness.'"[7]

The word "numinous," we are told, comes from the Latin *numen*, meaning supernatural divine power. It stands for "the specific non-rational religious apprehension and its object, at all its levels, from the first dim stirrings where religion can hardly yet be said to exist to the most exalted forms of spiritual experience."[8]

His translator, Dr. Harvey, Professor of Philosophy at Armstrong College, adds that there develops in man a "growing awareness of an object, deity . . . a response, so to speak, to the impact upon the human mind of 'the divine', as it reveals itself whether obscurely or clearly. The primary fact is the confrontation of the human mind with a Something, whose character is only gradually learned, but which is from the first felt as a transcendent presence, 'the beyond', even where it is also felt as 'the within' man."[9]

Through attention to life purpose, through concentration on life work, through keen interest in the sciences which engage the attention of our best minds, and through meditation, as practised by a few in the religious field, many have arrived at a point where two things happen: the idea of the holy, of Being and of relationship to that Being enter in as dominating factors in the life. Secondly, the mind

[7] Otto, Rudolf, *The Idea of the Holy*, p. 7.
[8] Otto, Rudolf, *Ibid.*, p. XVII of Translator's Preface.
[9] *Ibid.*, p. XV of Translator's Preface.

begins to demonstrate a new activity. Instead of registering and storing up in memory the contacts which the senses have communicated, and absorbing that information which is the common heritage of the day through books and the spoken word, it reorients itself to new knowledge and begins to tap new sources of information. Instinct and intellect have done their work; now the intuition begins to play its part.

It is to this point that the meditation work we have been considering has brought us and for which the education of the memory and the cataloguing of world knowledge has prepared us. They have had their day. For many thousands, therefore, a new endeavor is in order. Is it perhaps possible that for those souls now being born into world experience, the old education with its memory training, its books and lectures and its appropriation of so-called facts has become insufficient? For them we must either formulate a new method, or modify the present technique and so find time for the process of mind reorientation which will enable a man to be aware of more fields of knowledge than he now contacts. Thus we shall demonstrate the truth of the words of Mr. Chaplin in his valuable little book *The Soul*, that ". . . it is through Soul that bodily processes attain their significance."[10]

The conquest of the kingdom of the soul looms before man. The day when the word *Psychology* will return to its original meaning is at hand. Education

[10] Chaplin, F. K., *The Soul*, p. 63.

will then have two functions. It will fit man to handle his worldly contacts with the greatest efficiency and use intelligently that apparatus which the Behaviorists have done so much to explain, and it will also initiate him into the realm to which the mystics have always testified and to which the mind—rightly used—holds the key.

In the preceding chapter the method was dealt with through which a man could begin to be master of his instrument, the mind, and learn so to focus his thought upon a chosen theme or idea that he could close out all outer concepts and shut the door entirely on the phenomenal world. We shall consider the manner how he could carry his focussed thought higher and higher (to use the language of the mystic), until mind itself failed, and he found himself on a peak of thought from which a new world could be visioned. In the meditation process up to this stage there has been an intense activity, and no condition of quiescence, of negativity, or of passive receptivity. The physical body has been forgotten and the brain held in a state of positive receptiveness, ready to be swept into action by the mind when it again turns its attention downwards. We must remember that in using all such words as "upwards" and "downwards," "higher" and "lower," we are talking symbolically. One of the first things a mystic learns is that dimensions do not exist in consciousness, and that the "within" and "without," the "higher" and the "lower" are only figures of speech, by which certain ideas are conveyed as to realized conditions of awareness.

The point that we now have reached brings us to the verge of the transcendental. We proceed upon hypothesis. The tangible and the objective are temporarily forgotten and no longer engross the attention, nor is any form of sensation the aim. All manner of feeling must be, for the time, shut off. Petty annoyances and the like, along with sorrow, will be forgotten, and likewise joy, for we are not seeking the "consolations of religion." The attention is focussed in the mind and the only reactions recorded are mental. Thought has dominated the consciousness during the stage of "meditation with seed" or with an object, but now even this has to go. As one mystical writer puts it: "How shall I put mind out of mind?" For as my objective is neither sensation nor feeling, neither is it thought. Here lies the greatest obstacle to the intuition and the state of illumination. No longer is the attempt to hold anything in the mind to be prolonged, nor is there anything to be thought out. Ratiocination must be left aside, and the exercise of a higher and hitherto probably unused faculty must take its place. The seed thought has attracted our attention, and awakened our interest, and this has sustained itself into the phase of concentration. This again prolongs itself into contemplation, and the result of the latter is illumination. Here we have a brief summation of the entire process—Attraction, Interest,

Concentrated Attention and prolonged one-pointed Reflection or Meditation.

What have been the results of the meditation process up to this point? They might be enumerated as follows:

1. The reorganizing of the mind and its reorientation.

2. The centering of a man's attention in the world of thought, instead of on the world of feeling, and hence the withdrawal of the focus of attraction from the senses.

3. The development of a faculty of instantaneous concentration as a preliminary to meditation, and the capacity to focus the mind unswervingly upon any chosen subject. Evelyn Underhill defines this faculty as follows:

"The act of perfect concentration, the passionate focussing of the self upon the one point, when it is applied in 'the unity of the spirit and the bonds of love' to real and transcendental things, constitutes in the technical language of mysticism the state of meditation or recollection, and . . . is the necessary prelude of pure contemplation."[11]

III. *The Stage of Contemplation*

We are entering a realm of realization now which is much handicapped by two things: the use of words, which only serve to limit and distort, and the writings of the mystics themselves which—while they are full of wonder and of truth—are colored by the symbolism of their race and age, and by the

[11] Underhill, Evelyn, *Mysticism*, p. 58.

quality of feeling and emotion. The mystics, as a general rule, drift to and fro between moments of high illumination or of vision, and "the misty flats" of intense feeling and longing. They are either undergoing the joy and ecstasy of realization that lasts but a fleeting moment, or the agony of desire for the continuation of the experience. There seems (in the majority of cases) no sense of security or certainty of repetition, and only a longing for the attainment of such a state of holiness that the condition could be continuously present. In the ancient technique and the orderly meditation with which the East has lately dowered us, it seems possible that through knowledge of the way and through understanding of the process, the mystical experience may itself be transcended, and knowledge of divine things, and identification with the indwelling Deity may be brought about *at will*. The race now has the necessary mental equipment and can add to the way of the mystic that of the conscious intellect.

But between the stage of prolonged concentration, which we call meditation, and that of contemplation, which is of an entirely different category, there comes a transition period, which the Oriental student calls "meditation without seed," or, "without an object." It is not contemplation. It is not a process of thought. That is past, while the later stage is not yet achieved. It is a period of mind steadiness, and of waiting. Fr. Nouet describes this perhaps as well as anyone in the following words:

"When the man of prayer has made considerable progress in meditation, he passes insensibly to affective prayer, which, being between meditation and contemplation, as the dawn is between the night and the day, possesses something both of the one and of the other. In its beginnings it contains more of meditation, because *it still makes use of reasoning*; . . . because having acquired much light by the prolonged use of considerations and reasonings, *it enters at once into its subject*, and sees *all its developments without much difficulty*. . . . Hence it follows as it perfects itself it discards reasonings. . . . "[12]

The versatility of the rapidly moving and sensitively responsive mental substance can be brought, we have seen, into a stabilized condition, through prolonged meditation. This brings about a state of mind which renders the thinker unresponsive to vibrations and contacts coming from the outer phenomenal world and from the world of the emotions, and so renders passive the sensory apparatus, the brain and that vast inter-locking network which we call the nervous system. The world in which man usually functions is shut off, yet he preserves at the same time an intense mental attention and a one-pointed orientation to the new world in which that which we call the soul lives and moves. The true student of meditation learns to be wide awake mentally, and potently aware of phenomena, vibration and states of being. He is positive, active and self-reliant, and the brain and the focussed mind are closely co-ordinated. He is no impractical dreamer, yet the

[12] Nouet, Fr., *Conduite de l'Homme d'Oraison*, Book IV, ch. 1.

world of practical and physical affairs is temporarily negated.

If the student is not naturally of the positive mental type, some serious, persistent, intellectual training (designed to create mental alertness and polarization) should be taken up along with the practice of meditation, otherwise the process will degenerate into an emotional revery, or a negative blankness. Both conditions carry with them their own dangers, and, if prolonged, will tend to make a man an impractical person, impotent and inefficient in daily affairs. His life will become less and less useful to himself or to others. He will find himself dwelling more and more in uncontrolled irrational fancies, and emotional fluctuations. In such a soil the seeds of egoism easily sprout, and psychism flourishes.

The mind, therefore, positive, alert and well-controlled, is carried forward on the wings of thought and then held steady at the highest attainable point. A condition is then brought about in the mind which is analogous to one which has already taken place in the brain. It is held in a waiting attitude, whilst the consciousness of the thinker shifts into a new state of awareness and he becomes identified with the true inner and spiritual man. What is technically called the "perceiving consciousness" waits.

These two stages of meditation, one of intense activity and the other of an intense waiting, have been called the Martha and Mary states, and the idea, through this metaphor, becomes somewhat clearer. It is a period of silence whilst something inner transpires, and is perhaps the hardest part of the technique to master. It is so easy to slip back into the intellectual activity which ordinary meditation connotes, for one has not yet learnt to contemplate. Dr. Bennett describes this stage in some comments upon Ruysbroeck. He says:

"Ruysbroeck here distinguishes two marks of 'true' passivity: first, it is 'actively sought,' that is, a certain effort is necessary to maintain it. Second, it differs from any natural or automatic type of relief by the moral preparation which precedes it. . . . This enforced waiting, this self-imposed receptivity, which is the defining mark of the stage of contemplation, is not the end of the mystic's career. It is the end of his efforts, in the sense that he can do no more, but it is destined to give way to the stage of ecstasy when matters are taken out of the hand of the individual and he becomes the vehicle of a power greater than himself. 'Remain steadfastly in thyself until thou art drawn out of thyself without any act of thine'."[13]

He speaks later on in the same chapter of the breathless attention, the hard-earned and hard-held waiting for the divine revelation. The ancient sage of India, Patanjali, tells us the same thing, when he says that, when "the mind-stuff becomes absorbed in that which is the Reality (or the idea embodied in the form) and is unaware of separateness or of the personal self," this brings him to the stage of contemplation and he enters into the consciousness of the soul. He discovers that all the time it has been the soul which has lured him on into union with itself. How? Another Hindu teacher tells us that

[13] Bennett, Charles A., *A Philosophical Study of Mysticism*, p. 62.

"the soul has the means. Thinking is the means. When thinking has completed its task of release, it has done what it had to do and ceases."[14]

In contemplation, a higher agent enters in. *It is the Soul that contemplates.* The human consciousness ceases its activity and the man becomes what he is in reality—a soul, a fragment of divinity, conscious of its essential oneness with Deity. The Higher Self becomes active, and the lower or personal self is entirely quiescent and still, whilst the true spiritual Entity enters into its own kingdom and registers the contacts that emanate from that spiritual realm of phenomena.

The world of the soul is seen as a reality; the transcendental things are known to be facts in nature; union with Deity is realized as constituting as much a fact in the natural process as is the union between the life of the physical body and that body.

The man's consciousness, therefore, is no longer focussed in that waiting mind, but has slipped over the borderland into the realm of spirit and he becomes literally the soul, functioning in its own realm, perceiving the "things of the Kingdom of God," able to ascertain truth at first hand, and aware in full waking consciousness of its own nature, prerogatives and laws. Whilst the true spiritual man is thus active in his own nature and in his own world, the mind and brain are held steady and positive, oriented to the soul, and according to the facility with

[14] *The Vishnu Purana*, VI., 7, 90.

which this is done will be the capacity of both to register and record that which the soul is perceiving.

In meditation we endeavor to receive impressions from the inner God, the Higher Self, direct to the physical brain, via the mind. In contemplation a still higher stage is entered upon and we endeavor to receive into the physical brain that which the *soul itself perceives* as It looks outward upon those new fields of perception.

In the average man, the soul is occupied (as the Perceiver) with the three worlds of human endeavor, and looks out, therefore, upon the physical, emotional and mental states of being. The soul identifies Itself for aeons with the forms through which contact has to be made if those lower states of consciousness are to be known. Later, when a man has gained control of the mind and can offer it to the soul as a transmitting agent, then a vast region of spiritual awareness can unfold itself. The soul itself can then become a transmitting agent, and can pass on, via the mind and from thence to the physical brain, some of the realizations and concepts of the Spirit aspect. Students would do well to remember the words in *The Secret Doctrine*.

"Matter is the Vehicle for the manifestation of Soul on this plane of existence, and Soul is the Vehicle on a higher plane for the manifestation of Spirit, and these three are a Trinity synthesized by Life, which pervades them all."[15]

This, in the academic language of occultism, is the realization of the mystic. Cardinal Richelieu

[15] Blavatsky, H. P., *The Secret Doctrine*, Vol. I, p. 80.

calls contemplation that state "in which man sees
and knows God without using the imagination and
without discursive reasoning," and Tauler expresses
it thus:

"God desires to dwell in the superior faculties—the memory, the intellect, and the will, and to operate in these after
a divine manner. This is His true abode, His field of action;
it is there that He finds His likeness. It is there that we
must seek Him if we desire to find Him and by the shortest
way. Then the spirit is transported high above all the
faculties into a void of immense solitude whereof no mortal
can adequately speak. . . . When, afterwards, these persons come to themselves again, they find themselves possessed of a distinct knowledge of things, more luminous and
more perfect than that of others."[16]

Contemplation has been described, as a psychic
gateway, leading from one state of consciousness to
another. Jeremy Taylor calls it the "transition from
intense meditation to that contemplation which attains to the vision of the wonders of God, as the human soul enters the realm of the divine light."[17]
Francois Malaval, who lived and wrote in the 17th
century puts it most beautifully. He says:

"This act (contemplation) is also more perfect than
reasoning because in reasoning the soul speaks, whilst in
this act it enjoys. Reasoning . . . convinces the soul by its
principles, but here the soul is rather illumined than convinced, it sees rather than examines. Reasoning occupies
itself in the consideration of a word, a proposition, or a
discourse; but this simple sight of God, supposing all

[16] Quoted by Poulain, R. P., S.J., *Graces of Interior Prayer*, p. 272.
[17] Puglisi, Mario, *Prayer*, p. 181.

reasonings as things passed and known, contemplates its object in God Himself. . . ."[18]

Through this gateway of vision the man passes and finds himself to be the soul. From the vantage of the soul, he realizes himself to be the Perceiver, who can perceive equally the world of spiritual realities and the world of daily experience; he can look, if he so chooses, in either direction.

The problem is to acquire an equal facility in the work of perception on spiritual levels as we have learned on worldly levels, and one of the important points to remember is that in both cases the triplicity of soul, mind, and brain must play their part, but with a differing orientation and attention. It becomes simply a question of focus. The brain is active in practically a subconscious manner towards the instincts and habits which guide our physical plane life and appetites. Through right education, it learns to be receptive towards impressions emanating from the mind, and instead of being only a sensory register or recorder, it learns to respond to thought impressions. The mind in its turn has an instinctive tendency to record all outer information, but can be trained to be receptive towards the soul, and to register information coming from that higher source. In time we can acquire facility and practice in utilizing either brain or mind actively or passively, and eventually bringing about a perfect interplay between them and finally between the soul, the mind

[18] Malaval, F., *A Simple Method of Raising the Soul to Contemplation*, p. 102.

and the brain. We can sum up all that has happened during the three stages we have considered in the words of Patanjali—

"The gradual conquest of the mind's tendency to flit from one object to another (that is, concentration) and the power of one-pointedness (that is, meditation) make the development of contemplation."[19]

and when these three are simultaneously performed we are told that "this threefold power of attention, meditation and contemplation is more interior than the means of growth previously described." It is interesting to note that Malaval in his second Treatise, Dialogue III, makes the same point, linking faith, meditation and contemplation together as a synthetic act. The knowers in both the East and the West think alike.

Contemplation has been also defined by Evelyn Underhill in her most useful book, *Mysticism*, as the "lull between two activities." During this lull a new method of knowing and of being is instituted. This is perhaps one of the simplest and the most practical ways of understanding contemplation. *It is the interlude wherein the soul is active.* This soul activity is preceded by what we might call an upward activity. The physical brain has been quieted and held steady; the feeling or sensory apparatus has also been stilled and is no longer permitted to register information from its usual field of awareness; the mind has been focussed and held actively passive in the light which streams from the kingdom of the

[19] Bailey, Alice A., *The Light of the Soul*, III., 11.

soul. We refuse the passage of any information from the world of ordinary phenomena. This has been brought about through right concentration and meditation. This achieved, there ensues the interlude wherein the man knows himself to be a soul, dwelling in the eternal and freed from the limitations of form. This interlude is necessarily brief at first but as progress in control develops, it lengthens. The key to the whole process is the sustained concentration and attention of the mind "whilst the soul, the spiritual man, the perceiving being, contemplates."

In a former book I have dealt more fully with this use of the mind as the instrument of the soul, and will repeat one paragraph here:

"It should be made clear, however, that the perceiver on his own plane has always been aware of that which is now recognized. The difference lies in the fact that the instrument, the mind, is now in a state of control. It is, therefore, possible for the thinker to impress the brain, via the controlled mind, with that which is perceived. Man on the physical plane simultaneously *also* perceives, and true meditation and contemplation for the first time become possible. At first this will only be for a brief second. A flash of intuitive perception, a moment of vision and of illumination and all has gone. The mind begins again to modify itself and is thrown into activity, the vision is lost sight of, the high moment has passed, and the door into the soul-realm seems suddenly to shut. But assurance has been gained; a glimpse of reality has been registered on the brain and the guarantee of future achievement is recognized."[20]

[20] Bailey, Alice A., *The Light of the Soul*, III., 9.

The second activity concerns itself with a dual work carried on by the mind. Having been held steady in the light, it now records and registers the ideas, impressions and concepts imparted to it by the contemplating soul, formulating them into phrases and sentences, building them into thought forms and constructing clear mental images. It is for this that the need of a good mental apparatus will become apparent. A trained mind and a well-stocked memory and a carefully cultured mentality will greatly facilitate the work of the soul in gaining a right record and an accurate registering of its knowledge. Then, following upon this mental activity, will ensue a process of transmitting the gained information to the waiting quiescent brain.

When the soul has learned to handle its instrument, through the medium of the mind and the brain, direct contact and interplay between the two becomes increasingly possible and steady, so that a man at will can focus his mind upon earthly affairs and be an efficient member of society, or upon heavenly things and function in his true being as a son of God. When this is the case, the soul utilizes the mind as a transmitting agent and the physical brain is trained to be responsive to that which is transmitted. The true son of God can live in two worlds at once; He is a citizen of the world and of the Kingdom of God. I cannot do better than close this chapter with some words of Evelyn Underhill:

"The full spiritual consciousness of the true mystic is developed not in one but in two apparently opposite but really complementary directions. . . . On the one hand he is intensely aware of, and knows himself to be at one with that active world of becoming. . . . Hence though he has broken forever with the bondage of the senses, he perceives in every manifestation of life a sacramental meaning; a loveliness, a wonder, a heightened significance which is hidden from other men. . . . On the other hand, the full mystic consciousness also attains to what is, I think, its really characteristic quality. It develops the power of apprehending the Absolute, Pure Being, the utterly Transcendent. . . . This all-round expansion of consciousness, with its dual power of knowing by communion the temporal and eternal, immanent and transcendent aspects of reality . . . is the peculiar mark, the *ultimo sigillo* of the great mystic. . . .''[21]

The results of this dual activity and facility of interplay we will consider next. The intuition begins to function; illumination is experienced, and the life of inspiration, with its many special characteristics must be studied, and this we will attempt in our next chapter.

[21] Underhill, Evelyn, *Mysticism*, pp. 42-43.

INTUITION AND ILLUMINATION

"And God said:
Let there be light!
And there was light."

BIBLE

CHAPTER SEVEN

Intuition and Illumination

WE HAVE laid down the general premise that modern educational methods in the West have familiarized man with the idea that he possesses a mind; they have brought him to an appreciation of the intellect, so much so, that to many the achievement of intellectual ability is the consummation of the work of evolution. We have suggested further that when the eastern technique of meditation (with its stages of concentration, meditation and contemplation) has been applied by the western intellectual, the mind processes can be trained to reach their highest point of development and can then be superseded by a still higher faculty, that of the intuition. We have, in the West, noted also that the finest minds we have, through an intense interest and application, reach the same standard of achievement to which meditation brings the eastern aspirant to knowledge. But at this point the parallel breaks down. Education in the Occident fails to carry its exponents on into the realm of the intuition, or of illumination. In fact, we rather smile at the idea of an illumined consciousness and ascribe much of the testimony available to the hallucinations of the over-stimulated mystic or to the psychopathic cases with which our psychologists are constantly dealing.

But it can be proved, I believe, that the developed spiritual perception and an illumined intellect can be part of the equipment of the sane and balanced business man or scientist, and need not necessarily indicate a lack of psychic balance, or emotional instability. The light of illumination and of inspiration is quite compatible with the pursuit of one's daily occupations, and this has been told us for centuries in an ancient Chinese teaching, dating back to the eighth century:

"Master Lü Tzŭ said: When there is gradual success in producing the circulation of the Light, a man must not give up his ordinary occupation in doing it. The ancients said: When occupations come to us, we must accept them; when things come to us, we must understand them from the ground up. If the occupations are regulated by correct thoughts, the Light is not scattered by outside things, but circulates according to its own law."[1]

These characteristics of illumination and its results are to be found working out in the consciousness of the man who has progressed through the stages we have earlier outlined, and form the theme of this chapter. Illumination is a stage in the meditation process, for it entails careful control of the mind and a scientific approach to the subject; it is a result of the true contemplative state and of soul contact, and indicates, with its sequential effects, the

[1] Wilhelm, Richard, and Jung, C. G., The Secret of the Golden Flower, p. 57.

institution of the second activity of the mind, considered a few pages earlier.

According to the pioneers into the realm of the soul, the condition of illumination supervenes directly upon the stage of contemplation, and might be described, in its turn, as producing three effects: That of an illumined intellect, of intuitive perception, and an inspired life upon the physical plane of existence. This condition is recognized by all mystics, and by all writers upon the subject of the mystic revelation. The thought of a Light which enters in and which shines upon our way, the symbolism of an intense irradiation or blinding radiance which accompanies the phase of divine contact, are so general in their use that we have come to look upon them simply as something couched in mystical phraseology, which means relatively little more than an attempt of the visionary aspirant to express in words the wonders that he has sensed.

It seems, however, on investigation, that there is a good deal of meaning in this special terminology and these symbolic phrases. The uniformity of the language, the testimony of the many thousands of reputable witnesses and the similarity of the related occurrences seem to indicate something in the nature of a genuine phenomenal happening. Dr. Overstreet, in *The Enduring Quest*, mentions a large number of those great individuals for whom it is claimed that they were illumined, and points out that "these men do not reason their way to conclusions, although reason—the search for truth—apparently played a part in preparation for their final insight. In every case," he adds, "they experienced what, for want of a better term, we may call 'illumination'." He goes on to warn us also that "we may, to be sure, brush these experiences aside as aberrations. . . ." But he says "these men do not act after the manner of men suffering from an aberration. Out of them has come a great portion of the spiritual wisdom of the race. They are, as it were, among the illuminati of mankind. If 'by their fruits ye shall know them,' these men have shown fruits so far above the average as to make them spiritual leaders of mankind."[2]

The trouble has been that with the average mystic, though not with the outstanding figures to whom Dr. Overstreet refers, there has usually been an inability to define or express clearly this state of illumination. "The mystic," we are told in the Bampton Lectures for 1930, "cannot explain, but he knows that he has known and not merely felt, and often that knowledge remains an abiding possession which no criticism can touch . . . though the mystics seem to be unable to convey to others any body of truth which cannot be reached by more ordinary channels of experience and reasoning, it is nevertheless possible that the intensity of their special apprehension of reality may serve, as extreme cases serve to test the truth of some general geometrical theorem, to set our fundamental problem in a clearer light."[3]

[2] Overstreet, H. A., *The Enduring Quest*, pp. 238, 239, 240.
[3] Grensted, Rev. L. W., *Psychology and God*, pp. 203-204.

It is here that the East steps in and shows the system whereby illumination can be gained, and produces for our consideration an ordered process and method which carries man to the state of identification with the soul. It posits—as a result of that identification and its subsequent effects—an illuminated perception and an intuitive apprehension of Truth. It is, we are told in the eastern Scriptures, the mind that reflects the light and knowledge of the omniscient soul, and the brain that, in its turn, is illuminated. This is only possible when the interplay between the three factors of soul, mind and brain is complete. Patanjali tells us in his *Yoga Sutras,*

"The Lord of the mind, the perceiver, is ever aware of the constantly active mind stuff.

"Because it can be seen or cognized it is apparent that the mind is not the source of illumination.

"When the spiritual intelligence which stands alone and freed from objects, reflects itself in the mind stuff, then comes awareness of the Self.

"Then the mind stuff, reflecting both the knower and the knowable, becomes omniscient.

"The mind then tends towards discrimination and increasing illumination.

"When the means to union have been steadily practised, and when impurity has been overcome, enlightenment takes place, leading up to full illumination.

"The knowledge (or illumination) achieved is seven-fold and is attained progressively."[4]

Patanjali goes on later to point out that, after proper concentration, meditation and contemplation,

[4] Bailey, Alice A., *The Light of the Soul,* pp. 408, 409, 415, 416, 422, 178, 172.

"that which obscures the light is gradually re-moved, and he adds:

"When that which veils the light is done away with, then comes the state of being called discarnate (or disem-bodied) freed from the modification of the thinking prin-ciple. This is the state of illumination."[5]

It is perhaps possible, therefore, that when Christ enjoined upon His disciples that they should "let their light shine," He was not speaking symbolically at all, but was urging upon them the necessity of ar-riving at a state of freedom from the body conscious-ness in order that the light of the soul could pour through the mind into the brain and produce that illumination which enables a man to say: "In that Light shall we see light."

The way to that freedom has always been under-stood by the Christian Church and is called the "Way of Purification." It entails the purifying or rarefaction of the lower body nature, and the wear-ing away of the veil of matter, which hides the light within each human being. The veil must be pierced and there are many ways of doing it. Dr. Winslow Hall in *Illuminanda*[6] tells us of three ways,—the way of Beauty, the way of the Intellect, and the way of the Soul. Through beauty and the search for the reality which has produced it, the mystic forces himself behind the outer form and finds the good and the wonderful. Dr. Otto[7] deals with this in his

[5] Bailey, Alice A., *The Light of the Soul*, pp. 118, 240.
[6] Hall, W. Winslow, M.D., *Illuminanda*, p. 93.
[7] Otto, Rudolf, *The Idea of the Holy*.

exegesis of the faculty of "divination," that capacity to recognize with awe and wonder the essential holy and beautiful behind all forms. His chapter is well worth careful consideration. Thus the mystic "divines" (through the divine within himself) the reality which the veil of matter hides. This is the way of the senses. Then there is the way of the intellect, of the intense focussing of the mind upon a problem and upon the form aspect in order to arrive at the cause of its being. In this way, the scientists have made so much progress and have penetrated so far within the veil that they have arrived at a something which they call "energy". Dr. W. Winslow Hall defines the third way, as follows:

"The way of the soul is at once the oldest and the widest of the three ways . . . for the soul does more than pierce the veil of matter; it identifies itself both with the veil and with the Reality behind the veil. Thereby soul and veil and Reality are felt to be one."[8]

We are thus brought back to the idea of Wholeness and of Oneness with the Universe, which we touched upon earlier, and Dr. Hall adds that "I would define illumination as an overwhelming sense of oneness with The Whole."[9]

Let us attempt at this point to express as simply as possible where our conclusions have led us, and see what has happened to the man who has carried forward his education from the stage of memory training and the grasping of information to that of

[8] Hall, W. Winslow, M.D., *Illuminanda*, p. 94.
[9] *Ibid.*, p. 21.

a conscious use of the intellect and from then on into the realm of the conscious knower.

Through concentration and meditation he has achieved a large measure of mind control and learned how "to hold the mind steady in the light." The consciousness then slips out of the lower self (out of the realm of awareness of the brain and the mind) and the mystic passes into the contemplative state, wherein he functions as the soul, and realizes himself as a Knower. The nature of the soul is knowledge and light, and its realm of existence is the kingdom of God. All the time that this identification with the soul continues, the mind is held steady and refuses all response to contacts emanating from other states of awareness, such as those coming from the emotional and physical worlds. Absorbed in union with God, transported into the "Third Heaven" (like St. Paul) and contemplating the beatific vision of Reality, he knows nothing, sees nothing, hears nothing except the phenomena which are appropriate to the world in which he is living. But in that world, he hears, and sees, and knows; he becomes aware of Truth, unveiled and freed from the glamour which the veil of matter casts upon it; he listens to the Wisdom which is stored up in his own unfathomable soul, and is that Wisdom itself, for subject and object no longer exist for him: he is both and knows it. He enters into the Mind of God— that universal storehouse of knowledge whose door stands ever open to those individual minds which can be sufficiently quieted and controlled to permit of their visioning the door and passing through it. And still, throughout all this transcendental process, the mind has been held steady in the Light.

Presently, however, the contemplative state comes to an end, and the mind is swept into a renewed activity, an activity based on its reaction to the light, and on its power to register and record the information with which the soul seeks to dower it. The energies of the soul have been outward-going into the world of divine realities. Now the focus of attention changes, and Deity turns its eyes upon the waiting instrument, and seeks to impress upon it as much of its Wisdom and Knowledge as it is capable of receiving and reflecting.

There is an aptitude among those writers on mysticism who are concerned with the purely mystic way, and have not studied adequately the technique of the East, to confound illumination with feeling. Evelyn Underhill, for instance, says ". . . The illuminated state entails a vision of the Absolute: a sense of the Divine Presence: but not true union with it." "It is," she says, "a state of happiness."[10] The illumination of the mind with knowledge and with a realization of union with Deity and its apprehension of the laws which govern the spiritual realm may, ultimately, produce happiness, but that happiness is an after effect and not a part of the illumined state. True illumination is related to the intellect, and should be—in its purest aspect— divorced from feeling altogether. It is a condition

[10] Underhill, Evelyn, *Mysticism*, p. 206.

of knowledge, it is a state wherein the mind is brought into relation with God, and the longer that condition can be held free from emotional reactions, the more direct will be the communication between the soul and its instrument, and the freer from deterioration will be the imparted truths.

A comparison of the way of the Knower and the way of the mystic might be of value here. The mystic, especially in the West, gains his flash of insight; he sees the Beloved; he touches heights of awareness, but his approach, in the majority of cases, has been the *heart* approach, and has involved feeling, sensory perception, and emotion. The result has been ecstasy. His technique has been that of devotion, discipline, an emotional striving forward, the "lifting up of the heart unto the Lord," the "vision of the Beloved," and "the marriage in the Heavens," the pouring out of the love nature at the feet of the Beloved, and consequent ecstasy. Afterwards, if we are to believe the writings of the mystics themselves, there has followed a period of readjustment to the life of every day, and, frequently, a sense of depression and disappointment that the high moment has passed, coupled with an inability to speak with clarity of that which has been experienced. Then a fresh cycle of devotion and discipline is initiated, until again the vision is seen and the Beloved contacted anew. From certain angles the self-centredness of the Western mystic is notable, and his failure to use the intellect most remarkable. We must except, however, such mystics as Boehme, Ruysbroeck, or Meister Eckhart, in whose writings the element of the intellect is strongly stressed, and the quality of knowledge most apparent. Note what Meister Eckhart himself says:

"There is one power in the soul: intellect, of prime importance to the soul for making her aware of, for detecting, God. . . . The soundest arguments expressly state (what is the truth) that the kernel of eternal life lies rather in knowledge than in love. . . . The soul is not dependent upon temporal things but in the exaltation of her mind is in communication with the things of God."[11]

The Knower has a different method from that of the mystic. His is the directing of the intellect to the object of its search; his is the way of the mind, and its discipline and control. He steadies the mind; he stops its versatility and focusses it; he seeks out after God; he divorces himself from feeling and is not interested in his own personal satisfaction, for the mind is the "common-sense," and in its highest use is dowered with the faculty of synthesis, of Wholeness. He will, as Dr. Müller-Freienfels puts it, "no longer speak of '*his*' soul, but of the universal soul which manifests itself in him, and unfolds itself in him as in all other creatures, and will endure even though this illusion of individuality perishes. . . . He will live his life as 'life', that is, as self-realization and self-completion, with the consciousness that it is not merely his own self that is

[11] Pfeiffer, Franz, *Meister Eckhart*, pp. 114, 83, 288.

being realized and perfected, but the universe, the deity, of whom this apparent self is a part.''[12]

Personal feeling is ruled out. The aspirant masters the mind, holds it steady in the light and then sees and knows. Then the stage of ILLUMINATION follows. Meister Eckhart sums up the difference between the two ways as follows:

"Knowledge raises the soul to the rank of God; love unites the soul with God; use perfects the soul to God. These three transport the soul right out of time into eternity.''[13]

These distinctions should be carefully noted. For many at this time, the achievement of knowledge of God is of greater import than love of God. That they already possess; it is the background of their effort, but not of their present objective and discipline. For the vast and unthinking majority, it is perhaps true that the mystic way of love and devotion should be the goal, but for the thinkers of the world the attainment of illumination should be the goal of their endeavor.

In the truly illuminated man, we have that rare combination of the mystic and the knower; we have the product of the mystical methods of the East and of the West; we have the union of head and heart; of love and the intellect. This produces what, in the Orient, is called the Yogi (the knower of union) and, in the Occident, is termed the practical mystic —which is our rather unsatisfactory way of desig-

[12] Müller-Freienfels, Richard, *Mysteries of the Soul*, p. 336.
[13] Pfeiffer, Franz, *Meister Eckhart*, p. 286.

nating that mystic who has combined the intellect
with the feeling nature, and is, therefore, a co-ordinated human being—with brain, mind and soul
functioning with the most perfect unity and synthesis.

The illumination of the mind by the soul, and the
throwing down into the waiting and attentive
"mind-stuff" of that knowledge and wisdom which
is the prerogative of the soul, produce, in the truly
unified and co-ordinated man, results which differ
according to the part of his instrument with which
contact is effected. Leaving the subject of Union
and the growth of transcendental powers for later
consideration, we will confine ourselves to the direct
effects of illumination. We might, for the sake of
clarity, sum up these results as follows:

The effect on the mind is direct apprehension of
truth and direct understanding of a knowledge which
is so wide and synthetic in its grasps that we cover
it by the nebulous term, the Universal Mind. This
type of knowledge is sometimes called the Intuition,
and is one of the main characteristics of illumination. A second effect on the mind is responsiveness
to telepathic communication and a sensitiveness to
other minds which have achieved an ability to function on soul levels. I do not here refer to so-called
telepathic communication on psychic levels, or to
that between brain and brain in the ordinary intercourse of daily life, with which we are all familiar.
I refer to the interplay that can be set up between
souls, divinely attuned, and which has resulted in

the past in the transmission of the inspired utterances of the world, in the world Scriptures, and in those divine pronouncements which have emanated from certain great Sons of God, such as the Christ and the Buddha. Intuition and telepathy in its purest form are, therefore, two results of illumination upon the mind.

On the emotional nature, or, in the language of the esotericist, in the desire or feeling body, we have the registering of joy, of happiness, and the experience of ecstasy. There is a sense of completion, of satisfaction and a joyous expectancy, so that the world is seen in a new light and circumstances take on a happier coloring.

> "Heaven above is brighter blue,
>   Earth beneath is sweeter green,
>   Something lives in every hue
>   Christless eyes have never seen."

In the physical body there are certain most interesting reactions. These fall into two main groups: First, a stimulation to an intense activity, which has a definite effect upon the nervous system, and secondly, there is frequently the appearance of a light within the head, which can be seen even when the eyes are closed, or in the dark.

Dr. W. Winslow Hall, in his book on illumination, deals with this aspect of the light, and says in one place that he wishes to prove that "Illumination is —not only a psychological, but also—a physiological fact."[14]

[14] Hall, W. Winslow, M.D., *Illuminanda*, p. 19.

These results on the triple instrument—mental, sensory and physical—which we designate as a human being, are only manifestations of the same basic energy as it is transferred from one vehicle to another. It is the same divine consciousness making its presence felt in different spheres of human awareness and behavior.

Let us deal first with the mental reaction. What is this mysterious thing we call the intuition? It is interesting to note that the word is totally ignored in some books on psychology, and those often by the biggest men in the field. The intuition is not recognized. We might define it as direct apprehension of truth, apart from the reasoning faculty or from any process of intellection. It is the emergence into the consciousness of some truth or beauty never before sensed. It does not emerge from the subconscious, or from the stored up memory, racial or individual, but drops into the mind directly from the superconscious, or from the omniscient soul. It is immediately recognized as infallibly true and arouses no questioning. All sudden solutions of apparently insoluble or abstruse problems, and numbers of the great revolutionizing inventions, come under this category. Evelyn Underhill speaks of this in the following terms:

". . . this illuminated apprehension of things, this cleansing of the doors of perception, is surely what we might expect to occur as man moves towards higher centres of consciousness. His surface intelligence, purified from the domination of the senses, is invaded more and more by the transcendent personality, the 'New Man' who is by nature a denizen of the independent spiritual world, and whose destiny, in mystical language, is a 'return to his Origin'. Hence an inflow of new vitality, extended powers of vision, an enormous exaltation of his intuitive powers.''[15]

This immediate access to Truth is the ultimate destiny of all human beings, and it seems probable that some day the mind itself will lie as much below the threshold of consciousness as the instincts now do. We shall then function in the realm of the intuition and shall talk in terms of the intuition with as much facility as we now talk in terms of the mind, and endeavor to function as mental beings.

Father Maréchal, in *Studies in the Psychology of the Mystics*, defines the intuitive perception in these terms:

"Intuition—defined in a quite general manner—is the direct assimilation of a knowing faculty with its object. All knowledge is in some sort an assimilation; intuition is an immediate 'information,' without an objectively interposed intermediary; it is the only act by which the knowing faculty models itself, not on an abstract likeness of the object, but on the object itself; it is, if you will, the strict coincidence, the common line of contact of the knowing subject and the object.''[16]

One of the most notable and suggestive books on the subject of the intuition, and one which gears in amazingly with both the eastern and western positions, is entitled *Instinct and Intuition*, by Dr. Dib-

---

[15] Underhill, Evelyn, *Mysticism*, p. 311.
[16] Maréchal, Joseph, S.J., *Studies in the Psychology of the Mystics*, p. 98.

blee of Oriel College, Oxford. In it, he gives us several interesting definitions of the intuition. He remarks that "as sensation is to feeling, so intuition acts to thought, in presenting it with material,"[17] and he quotes Dr. Jung as saying that it is an extra-conscious mental process of which we are from time to time dimly aware. He also gives us Professor H. Wildon Carr's definition: "Intuition is the apprehension by the mind of reality directly as it is and not under the form of a perception or conception, (nor as an idea or object of the reason), all of which by contrast are intellectual apprehension."[18] The intuition, he tells us "is interested in purely intangible results and, if it disregards time, it is also independent of feeling."[19] In a particularly clear passage, he defines (perhaps unintentionally, for his theme is with other matters) the co-ordinated practical mystic or knower.

"... intuitive inspiration and instinctive energy are finally tamed and unified in the complete self, which ultimately forms one single personality."[20]

Here we have the mechanism guided and directed in its physical relations and reactions by the apparatus of the instincts, working through the senses, and the brain, and the soul in its turn, guiding and directing the mind through the intuition, and having its physical point of contact in the higher brain.

[17] Dibblee, George Binney, *Instinct and Intuition*, p. 85.
[18] Carr, H. Wildon, *Philosophy of Change*, p. 21.
[19] Dibblee, George Binney, *Instinct and Intuition*, p. 132.
[20] *Ibid.*, p. 130.

This idea Dr. Dibblee sums up in the words: "The point at which I have arrived is the definite acceptance of two distinct organs of intelligence in human beings, the thalamus, which is the seat of instinct, and the cerebral cortex, which is the seat of the allied faculties of intellect and intuition."[21] This position is closely paralleled with that of the Oriental teaching, which posits the functioning co-ordinating centre of the entire lower nature to be in the region of the pituitary body, and the point of contact of the higher Self and the intuition to be in the region of the pineal gland.

The situation is, therefore, as follows: The mind receives illumination from the soul, in the form of ideas thrown into it, or of intuitions which convey exact and direct knowledge, for the intuition is ever infallible. This process is in turn repeated by the active mind, which throws down into the receptive brain the intuitions and knowledge which the soul has transmitted. When this is carried forward automatically and accurately, we have the illumined man, the sage.

The second activity to which the mind responds as the result of illumination is telepathy. It has been said that "illumination itself may be regarded as the highest known example of telepathy; for throughout the blazing forth of that supreme enlightenment, the human soul is a percipient and the Father of Lights, the agent." The agent may work through the medium of many minds, for the world

21 Dibblee, George Binney, Instinct and Intuition, p. 165.

of the soul is the world of group awareness, and that opens up a field of contacts which is wide indeed. Not only is the soul of man *en rapport* with the Universal Mind, but also with all minds through which that Divine Purpose we call God may be working. In this way we can account for the coming forth of the steady stream of illuminated writings and of the world messages down the ages, which have guided the thoughts and destiny of men and brought them forward along the path of realization from the stage of animism and fetishism to that of our present concept of an immanent Deity. From the point of view of man and nature we have progressed to that of a divine Whole in which we live and move and have our being, and with which we are identified in consciousness. We know ourselves to be divine. One after another the Sons of God have entered into their heritage and found themselves sensitive to the world plan. They have, through steadfastness in contemplation, equipped themselves to act as interpreters of the Universal Mind and as intermediaries between the non-telepathic multitude and the eternal fountain of wisdom. To the illuminates of the world, to the intuitive thinkers in all fields of knowledge, and to the telepathic and inspired communicators can be traced the best that man now knows, the origin of the great world religions, and the triumphs of science.

This telepathic communication must not be confounded with mediumship, or with the mass of so-called inspirational writings, which are flooding our markets at this time. Most of these communications are mediocre in character, and carry nothing new, or any message which will lead man on another step into the New Age, or guide his feet, as he mounts the stair towards the Heavenly Places. The tapping of the sub-conscious, the enunciations of a worthy and high-grade mentality, will account for ninety-eight percent of the material now appearing. They indicate that man has achieved much, and that he is becoming co-ordinated. They do not indicate the functioning of the intuition, nor the activity of the faculty of spiritual telepathy. People need most carefully to distinguish between the intuition and instinct; between the intellect in its lower aspects and the higher or abstract mind. The line of demarcation must be preserved between the inspired utterances of a soul in touch with Reality, and with other souls, and the platitudes of a nice and cultured mentality.

The effect of the illuminative process on the emotional nature takes two forms—and, paradoxical as it may seem—two exactly opposite forms. It will produce in some types the quieting of the nature, so that all anxieties and mundane worries cease and the mystic enters into the peace that passeth understanding. He can then say:

"There is a flame within me that has stood
    Unmoved, untroubled through a mist of years,
    Knowing nor love nor laughter, hope nor fears,
Nor foolish throb of ill, nor wine of good.

I feel no shadow of the winds that brood,
 I hear no whisper of a tide that veers,
  I weave no thought of passion, nor of tears,
Unfettered I of time, of habitude.
I know no birth, I know no death that chills;
 I fear no fate, nor fashion, cause nor creed,
I shall outdream the slumber of the hills,
 I am the bud, the flower, I the seed;
  For I do know that in whate'er I see
  I am the part, and it the soul of me.''[22]

Contrariwise, it may produce the mystical ecstasy—that uplifting and outpouring of the heart towards Divinity, to which our mystical literature bears constant witness. It is a condition of exaltation and of joyous certainty as to felt realities. It carries its possessor forward on the wings of bliss, so that temporarily, at any rate, nothing can touch or hurt. Figuratively, the feet are fleet to speed to the Beloved, and the interplay between the Lover and the Loved One is great, but always there is the sense of duality, of something other or beyond that which has been reached. This must be held in consciousness as long as possible or else the ecstatic vision will disappear, the clouds will veil the sun, and the world, with all its cares, will obscure the heavens. We are told in *Mysticism* that ecstasy, physically considered, is trance. It is a state of rapture, and can be either good or bad. Evelyn Underhill quotes Father Malaval as follows:

[22] Muirhead, John Spencer, *Quiet* (*The Oxford Book of English Mystical Verse*), p. 629.

"The great doctors of the mystic life teach that there are two sorts of rapture which must be carefully distinguished. The first are produced in persons but little advanced in the Way, and still full of selfhood; either by the force of a heated imagination which vividly apprehends a sensible object, or by the artifice of the Devil. . . . The other sort of Rapture is, on the contrary, the effect of pure intellectual vision in those who have a great and generous love for God. To generous souls who have utterly renounced themselves, God never fails in these raptures to communicate high things."[23]

The same writer goes on to tell us what, psychologically, is ecstasy. "The absorption of the self in the one idea, the one desire, is so profound—and in the case of the great mystics—so impassioned that everything else is blotted out."[24] It will be noted how the idea of desire, of feeling and of duality characterizes the ecstatic condition. Passion, devotion and a rapturous going-out to the source of the realization are ever present, and a careful distinction has to be made by the experiencer or they will degenerate into morbidity. With this condition of sensory awareness, we have basically nothing to do. Our goal is the high one of constant intellection and steady mental control, and it is only in the early stages of illumination that this condition will be found. Later it will be seen that true illumination automatically rules out all such reactions. The soul knows itself to be free from the pairs of opposites— pleasure as well as pain—and stands steadily in

[23] Underhill, Evelyn, *Mysticism*, p. 431.
[24] *Ibid.*, p. 434.

spiritual being. The line or channel of communication eventually is direct and eliminative from the soul to the mind, and from the mind to the brain.

When we arrive at the physical level of consciousness and of the reaction to the illumination which is streaming down into the brain, we have two predominant effects, usually. There is a sense or an awareness of a light in the head, and frequently also a stimulation to an activity which is abnormal. The man seems driven by the energy pouring through him, and the days are all too short for what he seeks to accomplish. He finds himself so anxious to co-operate with the Plan which he has contacted that his judgment is temporarily impaired and he works, and talks, and reads and writes with a tireless vigor which does, nevertheless, wear out the nervous system, and affect his vitality. All who have worked in the field of meditation, and who have sought to teach people along these lines are well aware of this condition. The aspirant does enter the realm of divine energy, and finds himself intensely responsive to it; he senses his group relations and responsibilities and feels as if he must do his uttermost to live up to them. This registering of a constant pouring in of vital force is eminently characteristic, for the co-ordination between the soul and its instrument, and the subsequent reaction of the nervous system to the energy of the soul is so close and exact that it takes the man quite a little time to learn the necessary adjustments.

A second effect, as we have seen, is the recognition

of the light in the head. This fact is so well sub-
stantiated that it needs little reinforcing. Dr. Jung
refers to it in the following manner:

". . . the light-vision, is an experience common to many
mystics, and one that is undoubtedly of the greatest significance, because in all times and places it appears as the un-
conditional thing, which unites in itself the greatest power
and the profoundest meaning. Hildegarde von Bingen, a
significant personality quite apart from her mysticism,
expresses herself about her central vision in a quite similar
way. 'Since my childhood,' she says, 'I always see a light
in my soul, but not with the outer eyes, nor through the
thoughts of my heart; neither do the five outer senses take
part in this vision. . . . The light I perceive is not of a
local kind, but is much brighter than the cloud which bears
the sun. I cannot distinguish in it height, breadth, or
length. . . . What I see or learn in such a vision stays long
in my memory. I see, hear, and know at the same time, and
learn what I know in the same moment. . . . I cannot
recognize any sort of form in this light, although I sometimes see in it another light that is known to me as the
living light. . . . While I am enjoying the spectacle of this
light, all sadness and sorrow disappear from my memory. . . ."

"I know a few individuals who are familiar with this phenomenon from personal experience. As far as I have ever
been able to understand it, the phenomenon seems to have
to do with an acute condition of consciousness as intensive
as it is abstract, a 'detached' consciousness . . . , which, as
Hildegarde pertinently remarks, brings up to consciousness
regions of psychic events ordinarily covered with darkness.
The fact that, in connection with this, the general bodily
sensations disappear, shows that their specific energy has
been withdrawn from them, and has apparently gone toward heightening the clearness of consciousness. As a rule,

the phenomenon is spontaneous, coming and going on its own initiative. Its effect is astonishing in that it almost always brings about a solution of psychic complications, and thereby frees the inner personality from emotional and imaginary entanglements, creating thus a unity of being, which is universally felt as a 'release.' "[25]

These words any experienced teacher of meditation can unequivocally endorse. The phenomenon is most familiar and goes to prove surely that there is a close physical correspondence to mental illumination. Hundreds of cases could be proved, were people willing to relate their experiences, but too many refrain from so doing because of the mockery and scepticism of the man who knows little. This light in the head takes various forms, and is often sequential in its development. A diffused light is first seen, sometimes outside the head and, later, within the brain, when in deep thought or meditation; then it becomes more focussed and looks, as some express it, like a radiant and very brilliant sun. Later, at the centre of the radiance, a point of vivid electric blue appears (perhaps the "living light" referred to above) and from this a golden pathway of light leads out. This has sometimes been called "the Path," and there is a possibility that the prophet was not speaking merely symbolically when he said that "the path of the just is as a shining light that shineth more and more until the day be with us."

In this light in the head, which seems a universal accompaniment of the illuminative state, we have

[25] Wilhelm, Richard, and Jung, C. G., *The Secret of the Golden Flower*, pp. 104-105.

probably also the origin of the halo depicted around the heads of the illuminati of the world.

Much investigation remains to be done along this line, and much reticence and prejudice has to be overcome. But many are beginning to record their experiences and they are not the psychopathics of the race, but reputable and substantial workers in the varying fields of human endeavor. The time may shortly be with us when the fact of illumination may be recognized as a natural process, and the light in the head be regarded as indicating a certain definite stage of co-ordination and of interplay between the soul, the spiritual man, and the man on the physical plane. When this is the case, we shall have brought our human evolution to such a point that instinct, intellect and intuition can be used at will by the trained and fully educated man, and the "light of the soul" can be turned upon any problem. Thus the omniscience of the soul will be manifested on earth.

Let me close this chapter with some words written by a Hindu mystic and some by a modern Christian mystic, typical examples of the two points of view of the mystic and the knower. The Hindu says:

"They are called Brahmins only that have an inner light working in them . . . the human soul is a lamp not covered over with a bushel. The lamp emits not the rays of the flesh but the rays of mental light to illuminate all humanity and is therefore the channel for the world soul. The rays of mental light assist all humanity in its mental growth and expansion, and the lamp is therefore one of the Eternal

World Brahmins. It gives light unto the world but takes nothing that the world can give.''

The Christian writes:

> "I saw a life ablaze with God!
>   My Father, give to me
> The blessing of a life consumed by God
>   That I may live for Thee.
> A life of fire! a life ablaze with God,
> Lighted by fires of pentecostal love!
>   A life on fire! on fire with love for men
>   Lit by divine compassion from above.
> A burning life, which God can take and drop
> In house, or street, or whereso'er He will,
> To set some other life alight for Him
> And thus to spread the fire on further still.''

Then we shall have evidenced the final stage of the meditation process which we call Inspiration. To the possibility of such a life the Great Ones of the ages testify. They knew themselves to be Sons of God and they carried that knowledge down into full realization in physical incarnation. They are inspired Declarers of the reality of truth, of the immortality of the soul, and of the fact of the kingdom of God. They are lights set in a dark place to light the way back to the Father's Home.

THE UNIVERSALITY OF MEDITATION

"To every man there openeth
A Way, and Ways, and a Way.
And the High Soul climbs the High Way
And the Low Soul gropes the Low;
And in between, on the misty flats,
The rest drift to and fro.
But to every man there openeth
A High Way and a Low,
And every man decideth
The Way his Soul should go."

JOHN OXENHAM

The Universality of Meditation

We have outlined the method through which the mystic can become the conscious knower, and have defined the sequence of the development which eventually brings about illumination of the physical brain, and the living of an inspired life upon earth. We started with the man who, having exhausted the resources and the satisfactions of physical living and facing the inevitability of a great transition to another dimension of living, seeks the way to knowledge and certainty. He discovers—when he investigates with impartiality—that there have been at all times those who knew, those who had penetrated to the heart of the mystery of being, and who have returned carrying the assurance of the immortality of the soul, and of the reality of the Kingdom of God. They speak, likewise, of a method by means of which they have arrived at this apprehension of divine Truth, and of a technique which has made possible their transition out of the fourth into the fifth kingdom in nature.

We found that these illuminated men, right down the ages, testify to the same truth, and that they claim for this universal method that it brings them certain results that might be enumerated as follows:

First: They achieve direct experience of divine realities, of transcendental truths and of the supernatural world. These appear, when contacted, to be as much a natural process and as vitally a part of the evolutionary development as are any of the processes to which the sciences of biology, of physics or of chemistry bear witness. Just as these three great sciences are occult to, and practically unattainable by, the average grade school student, so the higher metaphysics is occult and unattainable, even to the academician who lacks the needed open-mindedness, the definite training and the equipment.

Second: Another development is the unveiling of the Self. Through the mental and spiritual education which advanced meditation practices confer, the problem of the psychologists as to the nature of the Self, the soul, the psyche, is solved, and the word can be resolved back into its original meaning—Psyche, the name of the soul. The process has been that of a gradual unveiling, and of a sequential approach nearer and nearer to the soul. The psyche emerges in its true being.

Back of matter, there can be found an immanent and potent factor which is responsible for the coherence of the form nature, and which constitutes the acting personality in the physical world. This can be regarded as the life aspect, and scholars are wrestling all the time with the problem of life, trying to arrive at its origin and its cause. More deeply seated still can be found the feeling, suffering, experiencing, emotional aspect of the Self, working through the nervous system and the brain, and governing most potently all activities in the world of human affairs. It feels pleasure and pain; it is engrossed with moods and emotional reactions to life, and with worries and desires of all kinds. This is the usual personal life for most of us, for we feel more than we think at this stage of human development. The reason for this is told us with clarity by Patanjali as follows:

"The sense of personality is due to the identification of the knower with the instruments of knowledge. . . . The illusion that the Perceiver and that which is perceived are one and the same is the cause of the pain-producing effects which must be warded off."[1]

We are told by him in another place that life experience and the process of physical plane living and feeling come from "the inability of the soul to distinguish between the personal self and the spirit. The objective forms exist for the use and experience of the spiritual man. By meditation upon this, arises the intuitive perception of the spiritual nature."[2]

Through this vital experience and through the process of sensory desire and subsequent awareness, the man exhausts that aspect of his nature and penetrates deeper until he arrives at a third factor, the mind. At this point of investigation man now stands, and the close consideration of the mental processes and the study of mind reactions, their causes and objectives, are engrossing the attention

[1] Bailey, Alice A., *The Light of the Soul*, pp. 115, 116.
[2] *Ibid.*, p. 239.

of psychologists everywhere. Amongst them are many schools of thought, holding widely opposing views, but that a something called the mind exists, and that it is increasingly influencing the race, is now universally recognized.

Whither do we go from this point? It has been a steady progression down the ages of the evolving human consciousness, and a steady growth of awareness of nature, of the world in which men live, and an increasing grasp of the Whole, until now the entire world is knit together through the radio, the telegraph and television. Man is omnipresent, and the mind is the main factor in the bringing about of this apparent miracle. We have arrived at an understanding of the laws which govern the natural world, and some of those which govern the psychical. The laws of the spiritual realm, so-called, remain to be scientifically discovered and utilized. A few have known them and spoken to humanity about them, but they are only utilized by the pioneering spirits of our race. Among these few who stand out as the eminent Knowers, are the Buddha, the Christ, Plato, Aristotle, Pythagoras, Meister Eckhart, Jacob Boehme, Spinoza—the list is long. We are now beginning to ask the pertinent question: Is it not possible that many hundreds now are at the point where they can co-ordinate the brain, the mind and the soul, and so pass through the portal of mental awareness into the realm of light, of intuitive perception, and the world of causes? From the standpoint of the mental world into which we have now penetrated, leaving behind us the veils of the physical body and the psychical nature, may we not be able now to pass on to our next evolutionary development? Having arrived at some understanding of the nature of humanity and the mind, can we not begin to grasp the nature of the intuition and to function in another kingdom in nature with as much realization and facility as we function as men? The Knowers say that we can, and they tell us of the way.

Third: In the language of some of the pioneers into the spiritual realm, the third result of meditation is that we find God. It is relatively unimportant what we mean in detail by that little word of three letters. It is but a symbol of Reality. Every world religion posits a Life that is immanent in form, and a Cause that has brought all things into being. Every human being is conscious within himself of the dim struggles (becoming more fierce as the intellect develops) to know, to understand, and answer the questions of Why and Wherefore. The majority of men, no matter what their theology, when they stand before the portal of death, assert their belief in the Father of Beings and accept the implications of that Fatherhood. Let us regard God as that "High and Unknown Purpose" which can be recognized as the sum-total of all forms which express the Life, of all states of consciousness, and as the Life itself; let us regard Deity as that in which we live and move and have our being, and which is working out through every form in nature (including the human form), His own inclusive and synthetic Plan. The Knowers tell us that when they have arrived, through a method at a Way, and through the following of that Way have entered into a new state of being, the Divine Purpose and Plan stands revealed to them. They can enter into active participation with it, and become conscious and intelligent workers on the side of evolution. They know what is happening, for they have seen the blue prints.

Fourth: In the words of all schools of mystics in both hemispheres, these results are summed up in the words: Union with God, or At-one-ment with Divinity. God and man are at-one. The Self and Not-Self are unified. Tauler expresses it thus:

"In this union . . . the man does not attain to God by images or meditations, nor by a higher mental effort, nor as a taste or a light. But it is *truly Himself* that he receives inwardly, and in a manner that greatly surpasses all the savour, all the light of created beings, all reason, all measure, all intelligence."[3]

All other factors below the spiritual reality are but ways to the centre, and must be entirely superseded in the contemplative state wherein the man slips out of the form consciousness into that of the spiritual reality, the soul. This, being a conscious indivisible part of the Universal Soul (paradoxical as those words may be), is devoid of all sense of separateness; hence the union with God is a realization of a fact in nature which has always been. The

[3] Quoted by Poulain, R. P., S.J., *The Graces of Interior Prayer* p. 80.

soul consciously knows itself to be one with God. With this idea in our minds and with an understanding of the part that intellection has played, the words of St. Paul take on a new clarity, when he says: "Let this mind be in you which was also in Christ Jesus, Who, being in the form of God thought it not robbery to be equal with God."

The results of this realized union (realized when in the contemplative state) is illumination of the mind and of the brain, provided that they have both been held positively steady and in a waiting condition. The illumination, when it has become frequent and, finally, when it can be drawn upon at will, produces eventually the life of inspiration.

If these stages are grasped and mastered and if the intelligent man or woman can be found willing to submit to the outlined technique, we shall have many coming forth as demonstrators of this divine science. The words that I used in my book, *The Soul and Its Mechanism*, will be found true that "there will emerge a new race, with new capacities, new ideals, new concepts about God and matter, about life and Spirit. Through that race and through the humanity of the future there will be seen not only a mechanism and a structure, but a soul, an entity, who, using the mechanism, will manifest its own nature, which is love, wisdom and intelligence."[4]

It is interesting here to note the uniformity of the teaching of all religions and races as to the technique of entrance into the kingdom of the soul. At a

[4] Bailey, Alice A., *The Soul and Its Mechanism*, p. 130.

certain point on the path of evolution, it would appear as if all ways converge and all pilgrims arrive at the same identical position on the Way. From this point of junction, they travel the same way, and employ the same methods, and use a curiously similar phraseology. That the time has come when this should be definitely realized becomes apparent when we note the wide study of comparative religion, and the interplay between the races. These two factors are steadily breaking down the old barriers, and demonstrating the oneness of the human soul.

Speaking generally, this Way is almost universally divided into three main divisions, which are to be seen, for instance, in the three great religions, the Christian, the Buddhist and the Hindu faiths. In the Christian church, we speak of the Path of Probation, the Path of Holiness, and the Path of Illumination. Dr. Evans-Wentz of Oxford, in his introduction to *Tibet's Great Yogi, Milarepa*, quotes a Hindu teacher in the following terms:

"The three chief Tibetan schools, to my mind, mark three stages on the Path of Illumination or spiritual progress. In the first, the devotee is subject to injunctions and prohibitions . . . i.e., 'bound by the ordinances'. In the second, he adheres to traditional ways . . . wherein the ordinary restrictions are to a certain extent relaxed, although the devotee is not yet altogether free. In the third, the Ādi-Yoga, when through *yoga* practices the Light is seen, there are no longer any restrictions; for the state of Buddha . . . has been attained. These three stages correspond, roughly speaking, with what the *Tantras* mean by the . . . State of the Animal-Man . . . State of the Hero, and State of the Divine or Enlightened."[5]

The Method in Tibetan Buddhism

In studying the life of Milarepa, the Holy One of Tibet, who lived in the eleventh and twelfth centuries, A.D., we find it claimed for him that he attained union through the method of discipline, meditation and practice, and, ultimately, Illumination. We read as follows:

"He was one, who, having mastered the mystic and occult sciences, had communicated to him . . . continuously the four blissful states of ecstatic communion. . . .

"He was one, who having attained to omniscience, all-pervading goodwill, and glowing love, together with the acquisition of transcendental powers and virtues, became a self-developed Buddha who towered above all conflicting opinions and arguments of the various sects and creeds. . . .

"He was a being most diligent and persevering in meditation upon the Rare Path. . . . Having acquired full power over the mental states and faculties within, he overcame all dangers from the elements without. . . .

"He was a being perfect in the practice of the four stages of meditation (analysis, reflection, fondness, bliss. These are the four progressive mental states, leading to complete concentration of mind, producing ecstatic illumination). . . .

"He was a most learned professor in the Science of the Mind, having proved the Mind to be, beyond dispute, the Beginning and End of all visible phenomena, both material and spiritual, the Rays whereof, being allowed to shine unobstructedly, develop themselves, as he knew, into the three-

[5] Evans-Wentz, W. Y., *Tibet's Great Yogi, Milarepa*, p. 5.

fold manifestation of the Universal Divine Being, through their own free, inherent power."[6]

Thus we have the same procedure—mental activity, contemplation, union and illumination.

The Method in Chinese Buddhism

One of the main contributions to the process of enlightenment is an understanding of the way in which the Buddha found the Light. It demonstrates in a most remarkable way the use of the mind to overcome ignorance and its subsequent futility to carry a man on into the world of Light and spiritual being. Dr. Suzuki, Professor of Zen Buddhism at the Buddhist College at Kyoto, tells us about it in the following illuminating paragraphs. He tells us that it was through "supreme perfect knowledge" that the Buddha arrived at the wisdom which changed him from a Bodhisattva into a Buddha. This knowledge is

". . . a faculty both intellectual and spiritual, through the operation of which the soul is enabled to break the fetters of intellection. The latter is always dualistic inasmuch as it is cognisant of subject and object, but in the Prajñā which is exercised 'in unison with one-thought-viewing' there is no separation between knower and known, these are all viewed in one thought, and enlightenment is the outcome of this. . . .

"Enlightenment we can thus see is an absolute state of mind in which no 'discrimination' . . . takes place, and it requires a great mental effort to realize this state of view-

<hr>

[6] Evans-Wentz, W. Y., *Tibet's Great Yogi, Milarepa*, pp. 32, 33, 35, 38.

ing all things 'in one thought'. In fact our logical as well as practical consciousness is too given up to analysis and ideation; that is to say, we cut up realities into elements in order to understand them; but when they are put together to make the original whole, its elements stand out too conspicuously defined, and we do not view the whole 'in one thought'. And as it is only when 'one thought' is reached that we have enlightenment, an effort is to be made to go beyond our relative empirical consciousness. . . . The most important fact that lies behind the experience of Enlightenment, therefore, is that the Buddha made the most strenuous attempt to solve the problem of Ignorance and his utmost will-power was brought forth to bear upon a successful issue of the struggle. . . . Enlightenment therefore must involve *the will as well as the intellect*. It is an act of intuition born of the will. . . . The Buddha attained this end when a new insight came upon him at the end of his ever-circulatory reasoning from decay and death to Ignorance and from Ignorance to decay and death. . . . But he had an indomitable will; he wanted, with the utmost efforts of his will, to get into the very truth of the matter; he knocked and knocked until the doors of Ignorance gave way; and they burst open to a new vista never before presented to his intellectual vision.''[7]

Earlier he points out that the attainment of Nirvana is after all essentially the affirmation and realization of Unity. In the same essays we find the words:

"They (Buddhists) finally found out that Enlightenment was not a thing exclusively belonging to the Buddha, but that each one of us could attain it if he got rid of ignorance by abandoning the dualistic conception of life and of the world; they further concluded that Nirvana was not vanishing into a state of absolute non-existence which

[7] Suzuki, Daisetz Taitaro, *Essays in Zen Buddhism*, pp. 113-115.

was an impossibility as long as we had to reckon with the actual facts of life, and that Nirvana in its ultimate signification was an affirmation—an affirmation beyond opposites of all kinds.'"[8]

The term Prajñā used above is very interesting. It is "the presence in every individual of a faculty. . . . This is the principle which makes Enlightenment possible in us as well as in the Buddha. Without Prajñā there could be no enlightenment, which is the highest spiritual power in our possession. The intellect . . . is relative in its activity. . . . The Buddha before his Enlightenment was an ordinary mortal, and we, ordinary mortals, will be Buddhas the moment our mental eyes open in Enlightenment.'"[9]

Thus we have the mind focussed and used to its utmost capacity, and then the cessation of its work. Next comes the use of the will to hold the mind steady in the light, and then—the Vision, Enlightenment, Illumination!

The Method in Hindu Yoga

The Hindus have analyzed the process of mental approach to Reality, and the part the mind should play, more clearly, perhaps, than any other group of thinkers. Shankarâchârya tells us that:

"The Yogi, whose intellect is perfect, contemplates all things as dwelling within himself (in his own 'Self,' with-

[8] Suzuki, Daisetz Taitaro, *Essays in Zen Buddhism,* p. 47.
[9] *Ibid.,* pp. 52, 53.

out any distinction of outer and inner), and thus, by the eye of Knowledge (Jñâna-chaksus, an expression which might be rendered fairly accurately as 'intellectual intuition'), he perceives (or rather conceives, not rationally or discursively, but by a direct awareness and an immediate 'assent') that everything is Âtmâ.''[10]

The Yogi, or the one who has achieved union (for Yoga is the science of union) knows himself as he is in reality. He finds, when ignorance gives place to transcendental awareness, that he is identified with Brahma, the Eternal Cause, the One and the Alone. He knows himself to be, past all controversy, God—God immanent and God transcendent. The seer goes on to tell us that

''He is 'the Supreme *Brahma*, which is eternal, pure, free, alone (in Its absolute perfection), incessantly filled with Beatitude, without duality, (unconditioned) Principle of all existence, knowing (without this Knowledge implying any distinction of subject and object, which would be contrary to 'non-duality'), and without end'.

''He is *Brahma*, by which all things are illumined (partaking of Its essence according to their degrees of reality), the Light of which causes the sun to shine and all luminous bodies, but which is not made manifest by their light.

''The 'Self' being enlightened by meditation . . . , then burning with the fire of Knowledge (realizing its essential identity with the Supreme Light), is delivered from all accidents, . . . and shines in its own splendour like gold which is purified in fire.

''When the Sun of spiritual Knowledge arises in the heart's heaven (that is to say at the centre of the being . . .), it dispels the darkness (of ignorance veiling the

[10] Quoted by Guénon, René, in *Man and His Becoming*, p. 254.

single absolute Reality), it pervades all, envelops all, and illumines all.''[11]

Father Maréchal tells us that the

''. . . psychological experience lived by the contemplative passes through the two phases of mental concentration and unconsciousness described by M. Oltramare, according to the *Sarvadarsanasangraha*: 'It is in two successive phases that the Yogi saps by anticipation the basis of further existences and effaces the impressions that determine the present existence. In the first it is *conscious* . . . ; thought, then, is exclusively attentive to its proper object, and all the modifications of the thinking principle are suspended in the degree that they depend on exterior things; the fruits it gains under this form are either visible —the cessation of suffering—or invisible—immediate perception of Being which is the object of the meditation. . . . The second period of Yoga is that in which it is *unconscious* . . . the thinking organ is resolved into its cause . . . the feeling of personality is lost; the subject who is meditating, the object on which his thought dwells, the act of meditation itself, make but one thing. . . .''[12]

Patanjali, the greatest teacher of the science of Yoga in the world, has summed up the final stages in his fourth Book in the following words:

''The state of isolated unity (withdrawn into the true nature of the Self) is the reward of the man who can discriminate between the mind stuff and the Self, or spiritual man.

''The state of isolated unity becomes possible when the three qualities of matter (the three gunas or potencies of

[11] Guénon, René, *Man and His Becoming,* pp. 256, 258, 259, 260.

[12] Maréchal, Joseph, S.J., *Studies in the Psychology of the Mystics,* pp. 312-313.

nature) no longer exercise any hold over the Self. The pure spiritual consciousness withdraws into the One.

"When the spiritual intelligence which stands alone and freed from objects, reflects itself in the mind stuff, then comes awareness of the Self. . . . The mind then tends towards . . . increasing illumination . . ."[13]

Here again the same idea. The use of the mind, final withdrawal from the mind consciousness, and the realization of unity. This tends to steady illumination.

The Method of Sufism

The writings of the Sufis are much veiled in imagery and symbolism and have a stronger sense of duality than perhaps any other religious esoteric system, except the Christian mystical writings. But there emerges even from them the same expression of truth and the same basic method. The following excerpts from the oldest Persian Treatise on Sufism will show. It is interesting to note that those writings persist the longest and show the most wide usefulness which come from those who are Knowers, and who can relate their experience of divinity in such a way that they can teach and outline, as well as declare and affirm.

"The first step in unification is the annihilation of separation because separation is the pronouncement that one has become separated from imperfections, while unification is the declaration of a thing's unity. . . . Accordingly, the first step in unification is to deny that God has a partner and to put admixture aside. . . ."

[13] Bailey, Alice A., *The Light of the Soul*, IV., 25, 34, 22.

"Our principles in unification are five; the removal of phenomenality, and the affirmation of eternity, and departure from familiar haunts, and separation from brethren and forgetfulness of what is known and unknown.

"The removal of phenomenality consists in denying that phenomena have any connection with unification or that they can possibly attain to His holy essence; and the affirmation of eternity consists in being convinced that God always existed . . . ; and departure from familiar haunts means, for the novice, departure from the habitual pleasures of the lower soul and the forms of this world, and for the adept, departure from lofty stations and glorious states and exalted miracles; and separation from brethren means turning away from the society of mankind and turning towards the society of God, since any thought of other than God is a veil and an imperfection, and the more a man's thoughts are associated with other than God the more is he veiled from God, because it is universally agreed that unification is the concentration of thoughts, whereas to be content with other than God is a sign of dispersion of thought. . . ."[14]

Again we find these words:

"One of the Shaykhs says: 'Four things are necessary to him who prays: annihilation of the lower soul, loss of the natural powers, purity of the inmost heart, and perfect contemplation.' Annihilation of the lower soul is to be attained only by concentration of thought; loss of the natural powers only by affirmation of the Divine Majesty, which involves the destruction of all that is other than God; purity of the inmost heart only by love; and perfect contemplation only by purity of the inmost heart."[15]

Thus again we have the same truth.

[14] Nicholson, Reynold A., *The Kashf Al-Mahjúb*, pp. 281, 282.
[15] *Ibid.*, pp. 302-303.

The Method in Christianity

It is, of course, easy to find many passages which link the way of the Christian Knower with that of his brother in the East. They bear witness to the same efficacy of method and they too use the intellect just as far as it will go and then suspend all effort whilst a new condition of being is instituted and a new state of awareness supervenes. St. Augustine says: "Just as that is ineffable out of which the Son leaps from the Father in the first procession, so there exists some occult thing behind the first procession, intellect and will." Meister Eckhart links himself with the Oriental Knowers in the following words:

"Intellect is the highest power of the soul and therewith the soul grasps the divine good. Free will is the power of relishing the divine good which intellect makes known to it. The spark of the soul is the light of God's reflection, which is always looking back to God. The arcanum of the mind is the sum-total, as it were, of all the divine good and divine gifts in the innermost essence of the soul, which is as a bottomless well of divine goodness.

"The soul's lower powers should be ordered to her higher, and her higher ones to God; her outward senses to her inward, and her inward ones to reason; thought to intuition, and intuition and all to unity so that the soul may be alone with nothing flowing into her but sheer divinity, flowing here into itself.

"When a man's mind has lost touch with everything, then, and not till then, it comes in touch with God.

"In this inflowing grace there forthwith arises that light of the mind into which God is sending a ray of his unclouded splendour. In this powerful light a mortal is as far above his fellows as a live man is above his shadow on the wall.

"The man of the soul, transcending his angelic mode and guided by the intellect, pierces to the source whence flowed the soul. Intellect itself is left outside with all named things. So the soul is merged into pure unity."[16]

Thus, the great schools of intellectual meditation (devoid in the final stages of feeling and emotion) all lead to the same point. From the standpoint of Buddhism, of Hinduism, of Sufism, and of Christianity, there is the same basic goal: Unification with Deity; there is the same transcendence of the senses, the same focussing of the mind at its highest point, the same apparent futility of the mind beyond that point to carry the aspirant to his objective; there is the same entering into the state of contemplation of Reality, the same assimilation into God, and awareness of identity with God, and the same subsequent Illumination.

All sense of separateness has disappeared. Unity with the Universe, realized Identity with the Whole, conscious awareness of the Self and assimilation in full waking consciousness with both interior and exterior Nature—this is the definite goal of the seeker after knowledge.

The self, the not-self, and the relation between the two, are known as one fact, without differentiation. God, the Father, God, the Son, and God, the Holy Ghost, are realized as working smoothly together as one Identity—the Three in One and the One in

[16] Pfeiffer, Franz, *Meister Ecl.hart*, pp. 338, 144, 66, 101.

Three. This is the objective of all the schools wherein the mystic transcends feeling, and even thought, in the last analysis, and becomes united with the ALL. Individuality, however, remains in consciousness, but it is so identified with the sum-total that all sense of separateness disappears. Naught is left but realized Unity.

THE PRACTICE OF MEDITATION

"It is to be noticed that the Doctrine of this Book instructs not all sorts of Persons, but those only who keep the Senses and Passions well mortified, who have already advanced and made progress in Prayer, and are called by God to the Inward Way, wherein He encourages and guides them, freeing them from the obstacles which hinder their course to perfect Contemplation."

MICHAEL DE MOLINOS, *The Spiritual Guide*

THE PRACTICE OF MEDITATION

UP TO this point our discussion has been academic and comparative, discursive and indicatory. The Way that many have trodden has been pointed out, and the Path to Illumination has been considered. Now it behoves us to apply ourselves to an understanding of the practical work that we ourselves can do. Otherwise the entire objective of our study of meditation will be lost, and we shall only have increased our responsibility, without having made any real advance upon the Way.

Two pertinent questions immediately arise and should receive attention.

First: Can anyone, who has the desire, profit by and master the technique of Meditation?

Second: The Knowers of the East gained Illumination by retiring from the world into seclusion and silence. Owing to conditions of life in our Occidental civilization, this is not possible. Can there be hope of success without this disappearance into the solitudes of the world, into the forests and jungles, and into monastic seclusion?

Let us take each question and deal with it. These two questions must be disposed of and answered before we can go on to outline meditation work and indicate the method which it is advisable to follow.

In replying to the first question, as to the general suitability of all aspirants for this arduous work, it should be remembered, at the outset, that the very urge itself to do so can be taken as indicating the call of the soul to the Path of Knowledge. No one should be deterred if he discovers that he lacks in certain essentials the needed qualifications. Most of us are bigger and wiser, and better equipped than we realize. We can all begin to concentrate at once if we choose. We possess a great deal of knowledge, mental power, and capacities, which have never been drawn forth from the realm of the subconscious into objective usefulness; anyone who has watched the effect of Meditation upon the beginner will substantiate this statement—often to the mental bewilderment of the beginner, who does not know what to do with his discoveries. The results of the first step in the Meditation discipline, i.e., of Concentration, are often amazing. People "find" themselves; they discover hidden capacities and an understanding never used before; they develop an awareness, even of the phenomenal world, which is, to them, miraculous; they suddenly register the fact of the mind, and that they can use it, and the distinction between the knower and the instrument of knowledge becomes steadily and revealingly apparent. At the same time there is also registered a sense of loss. The old dreamy states of bliss and peace, with which the mystic prayer and meditation had dowered them, disappear; and, temporarily, they experience a sense of aridity, of lack and of an emptiness which is frequently most distressing. This is due to the fact that the focus of attention is away from the things of the senses, no matter how beautiful. The things that the mind knows and can record are not yet registered, nor is the feeling apparatus making its familiar impacts upon the consciousness. It is a period of transition, and must be supported until such time as the new world begins to make its impress upon the aspirant. This is one reason why persistence and perseverance must play their part, particularly in the early stages of the meditation process.

One of the first effects of the meditation work is usually an increased efficiency in the daily life, whether lived in the home, the office, or in any field of human endeavor. Mental application to the business of living is in itself a concentration exercise and brings notable results. Whether a man achieves final illumination or not through the practice of concentration and meditation, he will nevertheless have gained much, and greatly enriched his life; his usefulness and power will be enormously increased and his sphere of influence widened.

Therefore, from a purely mundane point of view, it is useful to learn to meditate. Who shall say whether an increased efficiency in living and in service is not just as much a step on the path of spiritual progress as any of the visions of the mystic? The spiritual results of the mental application which our Western business world demonstrates may, in the last analysis, be as vital a contribution to the sum-total of spiritual endeavor as any effects which may be noted in the world of organized religious effort. Confucius taught us, centuries ago, that implements of civilization were highly spiritual in nature, for they were the results of *ideas*, and Hu Shih tells us in that interesting symposium, *Whither Mankind*, ". . . that civilization which makes the fullest possible use of human ingenuity and intelligence in search of truth in order to control nature and transform matter for the service of mankind, to liberate the human spirit from ignorance, superstition, and slavery to the forces of nature, and to reform social and political institutions for the benefit of the greatest number—such a civilization is highly idealistic and spiritual."[1]

Our idea as to what constitutes spirituality has steadily grown. Through the use of desire, feeling and the reactions of the emotional nature, we have seen many thousands of human beings arrive at the point where they have been driven to transmute desire into aspiration, feeling into sensitivity to the things of the spirit, and love of self into love of God. Thus the mystic emerges.

Through the use of the mind in the business world, in professional work, in science and in art, we have seen two amazing things occur: Organized big business, with its selfish interests and material ideas, has, notwithstanding, been brought to a condition where it is group-conscious; group interplay and the interests of the greatest number are being for

[1] Beard, Charles A., *Whither Mankind*, p. 41.

the first time seriously considered. These are purely spiritual results; they indicate a growing soul awareness, and are the faint indications of the coming brotherhood of souls. Applied science in all fields has now been so developed that it has entered the realm of energy and of pure metaphysics. The study of matter has landed us in the realm of mysticism and of transcendentalism. Science and Religion are joining hands in the world of the unseen and intangible.

These are steps in the right direction. When the mental faculties have been developed racially through our Occidental technique in the business world (a vast school of concentration), a transmutation analogous to that which occurs in the realm of the desire nature, must inevitably take place, and has frequently done so. The mind can then be reoriented to the truer and higher values, and focussed in a direction other than that of material living. Thus the knower will emerge.

Therefore, any one who is not purely emotional, who has a fair education, and who is willing to work with perseverance, can approach the study of meditation with good courage. He can begin to organize his life so that the first steps can be taken on the path towards illumination, and this organization is one of the most difficult of steps. It is well to remember that all initial steps are hard, for the habits and rhythms of many years have to be offset. But once these have been taken and mastered, the work becomes easier. It is far harder to learn to read, than it is to master a difficult book.

The ancient science of Meditation, the "royal road to Union," as it has been called, might equally well be entitled the science of co-ordination. We have already, through the medium of the evolutionary process, learnt to co-ordinate the emotional-feeling-desire nature and the physical body, so much so that the states are automatic and often irresistible; the physical body is now simply an automaton, the creature of desire—high or low—good or bad—as the case may be. Many are now co-ordinating the mind with these two, and, through our present wide-spread educational systems, we are welding into a coherent unity that sum-total which constitutes a human being: the mental, emotional and physical natures. Through concentration and the earlier aspects of the meditation work, this co-ordination is rapidly hastened, and is followed later by the unifying with the trinity of man of another factor,—the factor of the soul. This has always been present, just as mind is always present in human beings (who are not idiots), but it is quiescent until the right time comes and the needed work has been done. It is all a question of consciousness. Professor Max Müller in his book *Theosophy or Psychological Religion* says that:

"We must remember that the fundamental principle of the Vedanta-philosophy was not 'Thou art *He*,' but 'Thou art *That*!' and it was not Thou *wilt be*, but Thou *art*. This 'Thou art' expresses something that is, that has been, and always will be, not something that has still to be achieved, or is to follow, for instance, after death. . . . By true knowledge the individual soul does not become Brahman, but *is* Brahman, as soon as it knows what it really is, and always has been."[2]

St. Paul emphasizes the same truth when he speaks of "Christ in me, the hope of glory." Through the trained and focussed mind this indwelling Reality is known, and the Three in One and the One in Three are proven facts in the natural evolution of the life of God in man.

It becomes apparent, therefore, that the answer to our first question is as follows:

First: We accept the hypothesis that there is a soul, and that that soul can be cognized by the man who can train and control his mind.

Second: Upon the basis of this hypothesis, we begin to co-ordinate the three aspects of the lower nature, and to unify mind, emotion and physical body into an organized and comprehended Whole. This we do through the practice of concentration.

Third: As concentration merges into meditation (which is the act of prolonged concentration) the imposition of the will of the soul, upon the mind, begins to be felt. Little by little the soul, the mind and the brain are swept into a close rapport. First, the mind controls the brain and the emotional nature. Then the soul controls the mind. The first is brought about through concentration. The second through meditation.

Out of this sequence of activities, the interested investigator will awaken to the realization that there is a real work to be done and that the primary quali-

[2] Müller, Max, *Theosophy or Psychological Religion*, p. 284.

fication that he needs is *perseverance*. Here it might be remarked that two things aid in the work of co-ordination: First, the endeavor to gain control of the mind, through the endeavor to live a concentrated life. The life of consecration and dedication, which is so distinctive of the mystic, gives place to the life of concentration and meditation—distinctive of the knower. The organization of the thought life at all times everywhere, and, secondly, the practice of concentration, regularly, every day, at some set time, if possible, make for the one-pointed attitude, and these two together spell success. The former takes some time, but it can be entered upon at once. The latter requirement of stated concentration periods, can also be entered upon, but its success depends upon two things: regularity and persistence. The success of the former depends upon persistence largely, but also upon the use of the imagination. Through the imagination, we assume the attitude of the Onlooker, the Perceiver. We imagine ourselves to be the One who is thinking (not feeling), and we steadily guide our thoughts at all times along certain chosen lines, making ourselves think what we choose to think and refusing entrance to those thoughts we choose to exclude, not by the method of inhibition, but by the method of a dynamic interest in something else. We refuse to permit our minds to range the world at will, or to be swung into activity by our feelings and emotions, or by the thought currents in the world around us. We force ourselves to pay attention to all that we do, whether it is reading a book, going about our business in home or office, social life or profession, talking to a friend, or whatever may be the activity of the moment. Should the occupation be such that it can be carried forward instinctively and call for no active use of thought, we can choose a line of mental activity or chain of reasoning and follow it out understandingly, whilst our hands or eyes are busy with the work to be done.

True concentration grows out of a concentrated, thought-governed life, and the first step for the aspirant is to begin to organize his daily life, regulate his activities, and become focussed and one-pointed in his manner of living. This is possible to all who care enough to make the needed effort and who can carry it forward with perseverance. This is the first and basic essential. When we can organize and rearrange our lives, we prove our mettle and the strength of our desire. It will be seen, therefore, that no neglect of duty is possible to the one-pointed man. His duties to family and friends and to his business or profession will be more perfectly and efficiently performed, and he will find time for the added duties that his spiritual aspiration confer, because he is beginning to eliminate the non-essentials out of his life. No obligation will be evaded, for the focussed mind will enable a man to do more in a shorter time than heretofore and to get better results from his efforts. People who are governed by their emotions waste much time and energy, and accomplish less than the mentally focussed person;

it is far easier for an individual who has been trained in business methods and who has risen to the rank of an executive, to practise meditation, than it is for the unthinking mechanical worker, or for the woman who is living a purely social or family life. These last have to learn to organize their days and leave out the non-essential activities. They are the ones who are always too busy to do anything, and to whom the finding of twenty minutes each day for meditation or an hour for study presents insuperable difficulties. They are so busy with the social amenities, with the mechanics of housekeeping, with a multitude of petty activities and pointless conversations that they fail to realize that the practice of concentration will enable them to do all they have hitherto done and more, and do it better. The trained executive, with a busy and full life, seems to find it much easier to obtain the extra time required for the soul. He has always time for the one thing more. He has learned to concentrate, and, frequently, to meditate; all that he needs to do is to change the focus of attention.

The answer to the second question as to the necessity to withdraw into the solitudes in order to evoke the soul opens up one or two interesting considerations. It would appear from the study of conditions that the modern western aspirant has either to forego the culture of the soul nature until such time as he can conform to the ancient rule of withdrawal, or he has to formulate a new method and take a new position. Few of us are so situated that we can renounce our families and responsibilities and disappear from the world of men to meditate and seek illumination under our particular Bo tree. We live in the midst of a thronging multitude and a chaotic situation which makes all vision of environing peace and quiet utterly out of the question. Is the problem then insuperable? Is there no way of overcoming the difficulty? Have we to renounce all hope of illumination because we cannot (from circumstances and climate, and from economic causes) disappear from the world of men and seek the kingdom of the soul?

Undoubtedly the solution does not lie in renunciation of the possibilities to which men in earlier races and centuries bear witness. It lies in a right understanding of our problem and of the privilege which is ours in demonstrating a newer aspect of the old truth. We belong, in the West, to a younger race. In the old, old East, the few adventurous pioneers sought seclusion and ascertained for us the opportunities, and safeguarded for us the rules. They held in safety for us the technique until such time as the masses of men were ready for a move forward in their numbers, and not in their ones and twos. That time has now come. In the stress and stir of modern living, in the jungles of our great cities, in the roar and bustle of daily life and intercourse, men and women everywhere can and do find the centre of peace within themselves, and they can and do enter into that state of silent positive concentration which enables them to reach the same goal, and attain the same knowledge, and enter into the same

Light to which the great Individuals of the race have borne witness. The secluded point to which a man withdraws, he finds to lie within himself; the silent place in which the life of the soul is contacted is that point within the head where soul and body meet, that region we earlier referred to where the light of the soul and the life of the body merge and blend. The man who can train himself to be sufficiently one-pointed can withdraw his thought at any time and in any place to a centre within himself, and in this centre within the head the great work of at-one-ment is carried forward. It involves a more dynamic attention and a more powerful meditation, but the race has progressed and grown in mental power and strength within the past three thousand years and can do what was not possible to the seers of old.

A third question arises at this point: What really happens to the aspirant, psychologically and physiologically, in meditation? The answer is: A great deal. Psychologically speaking, the mind becomes controlled, and passes under the domination of the soul; at the same time there is no negation of the ordinary mental faculties. They can be used more easily and the mind is keener than ever before. There is a capacity to think with clarity. The aspirant discovers that besides being able to record impressions from the phenomenal world, he is able to register also impressions from that of spirit. He is mental in two directions, and the mind becomes a cohering, unifying agency. The emotional nature, in its turn is controlled by the mind, and is rendered still and untroubled, and, therefore, presents no barrier to the inflow of spiritual knowledge to the brain. When these two effects have been produced certain changes take place in the mechanism of thought and awareness in the human head—so the eastern knowers tell us, and so the evidence seems to indicate. Advanced thinkers in the West, as we have seen earlier in this book, place the higher mental faculties and the seat of the intuition in the higher brain, and the lower mental faculties and the higher emotional reactions in the lower brain. This is in line with the eastern teaching that the soul (with the higher knowledge and the faculty of intuitional perception) has its seat in a centre of force in the region of the pineal gland, whereas the personality has its seat in a centre of force in the region of the pituitary body.

The hypothesis upon which the newer school in the educational field will eventually proceed (if the theories propounded in this book have any basis in fact) might be expressed in the following propositions:

One: The centre of energy through which the soul works is in the upper brain. During meditation, if effective, energy from the soul pours into the brain, and has a definite effect upon the nervous system. If, however, the mind is not controlled and the emotional nature dominates (as in the case of the pure mystic) the effect makes itself felt primarily in the feeling apparatus, the emotional states of being.

When the mind is the dominant factor, then the thought apparatus, in the higher brain, is swung into an organized activity. The man acquires a new capacity to think clearly, synthetically and potently as he discovers new realms of knowledge.

Two: In the region of the pituitary body, we have the seat of the lower faculties, when co-ordinated in the higher type of human being. Here they are co-ordinated and synthesized, and—as we have been told by certain reputable schools of psychologists and endocrinologists—here are to be found the emotions and the more concrete aspects of the mind (growing out of racial habits and inherited instincts, and, hence, calling for no exercise of the creative or higher mind). This was the theme of my earlier book, *The Soul and Its Mechanism,* and cannot be enlarged upon here.

Three: When the personality—the sum-total of physical, emotional and mental states—is of a high order, then the pituitary body functions with increased efficiency, and the vibration of the centre of energy in its neighborhood becomes very powerful. It should be noted that according to this theory, when the personality is of a low order, when the reactions are mainly instinctual and the mind is practically non-functioning, then the centre of energy is in the neighborhood of the solar plexus, and the man is more animal in nature.

Four: The centre in the region of the pineal gland, and the higher brain, are brought into activity through learning to focus the attentive consciousness in the head. In the Oriental books this is called by the interesting term "right withdrawal" or "right abstraction." This means the development of the capacity to subjugate the outward-going tendencies of the five senses. So the aspirant is taught the right withdrawal or abstraction of the consciousness which is outgoing towards the world of phenomena, and must learn to centre his consciousness in the great central station in the head from whence energy can be consciously distributed as he participates in the great work, from whence he can make a contact with the realm of the soul, and in which he can receive the messages and impressions which emanate from that realm. This is a definite stage of achievement and is not simply a symbolic way of expressing one-pointed interest.

The various avenues of sense perception are brought into a quiescent condition. The consciousness of the real man no longer surges outwards along its five avenues of contact. The five senses are dominated by the sixth sense, the mind, and all the consciousness and the perceptive faculty of the aspirant is synthesized in the head, and turns inward and upward. The psychic nature is thereby subjugated and the mental plane becomes the field of man's activity. This withdrawal or abstracting process proceeds in stages:

1. The withdrawal of the physical consciousness, or perception through hearing, touch, sight, taste and smell. These modes of perception become temporarily dormant, and man's perception becomes sim-

ply mental and the brain consciousness is all that is active on the physical plane.

2. The withdrawal of the consciousness into the region of the pineal gland, so that man's point of realization is centralized in the region between the middle of the forehead and the pineal gland.[3]

Five: When this has been done, and the aspirant is acquiring the ability so to focus in the head, the result of this process of abstraction is as follows:

The five senses are being steadily synthesized by the sixth sense, the mind. This is the co-ordinating factor. Later it is realized that the soul has an analogous function. The threefold personality is thus brought into a direct line of communication with the soul, and the man, therefore, in time becomes unconscious of the limitations of the body nature, and the brain can be directly impressed by the soul, via the mind. The brain consciousness is held in a positive waiting condition with all its reactions to the phenomenal world utterly, though temporarily, inhibited.

Sixth: The high grade intellectual personality, with its focus of attention in the region of the pituitary body, begins to vibrate in unison with the higher centre in the region of the pineal gland. Then a magnetic field is set up between the positive soul aspect and the waiting personality which is rendered receptive by the process of focussed attention. Then the light, we are told, breaks forth, and we have the illumined man, and the appearance of the phenome-

[3] Bailey, Alice A., *The Light of the Soul*, pp. 229, 230.

nal light in the head. All this is the result of a disciplined life, and the focussing of the consciousness in the head. This is, in its turn, brought about through the attempt to be concentrated in the daily life, and also through definite concentration exercises. These are followed by the effort to meditate, and later—much later—the power to contemplate makes itself felt.

This is a brief summation of the mechanics of the process, and is necessarily terse and incomplete. These ideas have to be accepted tentatively, however, before there can be an intelligent approach to the meditation work. It is as justifiable to accept such an hypothesis as the above as to accept any hypothesis, as a working basis for investigation and conduct. It is perhaps more justifiable, for so many thousands have proceeded upon these assumptions, have fulfilled the needed requirements, and—as a result—have changed assumption into certainty and reaped the reward of open-mindedness, persistence, and investigation.

Having formulated our hypothesis and accepted it temporarily we proceed with the work, until it proves false, or until our attention is no longer engaged. An hypothesis is not necessarily false because it fails to prove itself in the time we deem proper. People frequently give up their pursuit in this field of knowledge because they lack the needed perseverance, or their interest becomes engaged elsewhere. However, we are determined to go forward with our investigation and give the ancient techniques and formulas time to prove themselves. We proceed, therefore, to comply with the first requirements and endeavor to bring to bear upon life a more concentrated attitude of mind, and to practice daily meditation and concentration. If we are beginners, or are possessed of an unorganized mind, fluidic, versatile and unstable, we start in to practice concentration. If we are trained intellectuals, or have the focussed attentiveness that business training confers, we need only to reorient the mind to a new field of awareness and begin truly to meditate. It is easy to teach meditation to the interested business executive.

Next, the regular meditation work is attempted, and a certain time is set apart each day for this particular work. At the beginning fifteen minutes is ample time, and no more should be attempted for a year at least. May it not be truly said, if any one claims not to be able to find fifteen minutes out of the one thousand four hundred and forty minutes which constitute a day, that they are not interested? Fifteen minutes can always be found, if the will is on the side of the effort; it is always possible to rise fifteen minutes earlier every morning, or to forego that early morning gossip with the family, or to take the needed time from a book, or the movies, or from another gossip later on in the day. Let us be truthful with ourselves, and recognize things for what they are. The plea, "I have no time," is an utterly futile one, and indicates simply lack of interest. Let us consider now the rules upon which we will proceed.

First of all, we shall endeavor to find time early in the morning for our meditation work. The reason for this is, that after we have participated in the happenings of the day and in the general give and take of life, the mind is in a state of violent vibration; this is not the case if the meditation is performed first thing in the morning. Then it is relatively quiet, and the mind can be more rapidly attuned to the higher states of consciousness. Again, if we start the day with the focussing of our attention on spiritual things and on the affairs of the soul, we shall live the day in a different manner. If this becomes a habit, we shall soon find our reactions to the affairs of life changing and that we are beginning to think the thoughts that the soul thinks. It then becomes the process of the working of a law, for "as a man thinketh so is he."

Next, we shall endeavor to find a place that is really quiet and free from intrusion. I do not mean quiet in the sense of freedom from noise, for the world is full of sounds and as we grow in sensitiveness we are apt to find it fuller than we thought, but free from personal approach and the calls of other people. I should like here to point out an attitude which the beginner should assume. It is the attitude of *silence*. Aspirants to meditation talk much about the opposition they meet from their family and friends; the husband objects to his wife meditating, or vice versa; sons and daughters are inconsiderate and thoughtless in interrupting the devotions of the parent; friends are unsympathetic at the attempts. In the majority of cases this is the fault of the aspirant himself, and women are the worst offenders in this respect. People talk too much. It is nobody's business what we do with fifteen minutes of our time every morning, and there is no need to talk about it to our households, or to enjoin upon them that they must be quiet because we want to meditate. This will inevitably evoke a wrong reaction. Let us say nothing about the way we are seeking to unfold the spiritual consciousness; that is entirely our own affair. Let us keep silent about what we are doing; let us keep our books and papers shut away from people, and not litter up the family sitting room with a lot of literature in which they are not the least interested. If it is impossible to get a moment for meditation before the family disperses for the day's work, or before we ourselves betake ourselves to our business, let us find some time for it later on in the day. There is always a way to be found out of a difficulty, if we want a thing badly enough, and a way that involves no omission of duty or of obligation. It simply involves organization and silence.

Then, having found the time and the place, we shall sit down in a comfortable chair and begin to meditate. The questions then arise: How shall we sit? Is the cross-legged attitude the best, or shall we kneel, or sit, or stand? The easiest and most normal position is the best always. The cross-legged attitude has been, and still is, much used in the Orient, and many books have been written upon the postures, of which there are approximately eighty. But because it has been done in the past, and in the East, is no indication that it is the best for us in the present and in the West. These postures are the remains of a day when the race was being trained psychologically and emotionally, and much resemble the discipline that we impose upon a child when we set it in a corner and tell it to keep quiet. Some of the postures have relation also to the nervous body and that inner structure of fine nerves, called by the Hindus, the nadis, which underlie the nervous system as recognized in the West.

The trouble with such postures is that they lead to two rather undesirable reactions; they lead a man to concentrate the mind upon the mechanics of the process and not upon the goal, and, secondly, they frequently lead to a delightful sense of superiority, that has its basis in our attempt to do something that the majority is not doing, and which sets us apart as potential knowers. We become engrossed with the form side of meditation and not with the Originator of the form; we are occupied with the Not-self instead of with the Self. Let us choose that posture that enables us, the most easily, to forget that we have a physical body. This is probably for the Westerner the sitting attitude; the main requirements are that we should sit erect, with the spine in a straight line; that we should sit relaxed (without slumping) so that there is no tenseness anywhere in the body, and that we should drop the chin somewhat, so as to release any tension in the back of the neck. Many people sit, when meditating, gazing at the ceiling with tightly closed eyes, as if the soul was up above somewhere; they look as if they had swallowed the poker, and their teeth are often tightly clenched (perhaps to prevent some inspired utterance escaping them, which must have dropped from the soul). The whole body is poised and tense and tightly locked. They are then surprised when nothing occurs, except fatigue and headaches. The withdrawal of the consciousness from the channels of the senses does not involve the withdrawal of the blood in the body to the head, or the uncontrolled speeding up of the nervous reactions. Meditation is an interior act, and can only be performed successfully when the body is relaxed, rightly poised and then forgotten.

The hands should be folded in the lap, and the feet crossed. If the western scientist is right when he tells us that the human body is really an electric battery, then perhaps his Oriental brother is also right when he says that in meditation there is a bringing together of negative and positive energy, and that by this means we produce the light in the head. Therefore, it is wise to close the circuit.

Having attained to physical comfort, relaxation, and having withdrawn ourselves from the body consciousness, we next note our breathing and ascertain whether it is quiet, even and rhythmic. I would like here to sound a note of warning as to the practice of breathing exercises, except by those who have first given years to right meditation and to purification of the body nature. Where experience and purity are not present, the practice of breathing exercises entails very real dangers. It is impossible to put this too strongly. There are many schools giving breathing instruction at this time, and many exponents of breathing as a means to spiritual development. It has nothing whatever to do with spiritual development. It has much to do with psychical development, and its practice leads to much difficulty and danger. It is possible for instance, to become clairaudient or clairvoyant through the practice of certain breathing exercises, but where there is no true understanding of the process or right control by the mind of the "versatile psychic nature", the practicer has only succeeded in forcing entrance into new fields of phenomena. He has developed faculties he is totally unable to control, and he finds very often that he is unable to shut out sounds and sights which he has learned to register and being helpless to escape from the contacts of both the physical and the psychical, he is torn in two directions, and gets no peace. Physical sounds and sights are his normal heritage, and naturally make their impacts upon his senses, but when the psychic world—with its own sights and sounds—also makes an impact he is helpless; he cannot shut his eyes and remove himself from undesirable psychic surroundings.

A Doctor of Divinity and pastor of a large church wrote me not long ago that he had been taking breathing exercises, with the idea of improving his health, from a teacher who had come to his city. The result of his well-intentioned ignorance was that he opened up the inner hearing in the psychic sense. He said in his letter to me, "As I write to you upon my typewriter I can hear all sorts of voices and words and sounds which are not physical. I cannot stop them and I fear for my mind. Won't you please tell me what I ought to do to tune them out?" During the past ten years, many hundreds of people have come to me, asking for help, owing to the effects of indiscriminate following of the advice of teachers of breathing. They are quite desperate and frequently are in a serious psychic condition. Some we can help. Some few for whom we can do nothing end in asylums for the insane or in sanatoriums for the unbalanced. Much experience of these cases leads me to sound this warning, for in the majority of cases of uncontrolled psychic troubles, the cause is breathing exercises.

In the ancient teachings of the East, the control of the breath was only permitted after the first three "means to union," as they are called, had been somewhat wrought out in the life. These "means" are: First, the five commandments. These are, harmlessness, truth to all beings, abstention from theft, from incontinence, and from avarice. Second, the five rules, which are internal and external purification, contentment, fiery aspiration, spiritual reading, and devotion. Third, right poise. When a person is harmless in thought and word and deed, when he is unselfish and knows the meaning of poise—emotional as well as physical posture—then indeed he may practice breathing exercises, under proper instruction, and practice them with security. Even then he will only succeed in unifying the vital energies of the body, and in becoming a conscious psychic, but this may have its place and purpose, if he classes himself as a research experimenter.

Failure to conform to the necessary preliminary steps has landed many a worthy investigator in trouble. It is dangerous for an emotional and weak person to take breathing exercises in order to hasten development, and any teacher who seeks to teach these exercises to large groups, as is frequently done, is laying up trouble for himself and his followers. It is only here and there that, in the ancient days, the teachers picked a man for this form of tuition, and it was added to a training which had produced a certain measure of soul contact, so that the soul could guide the energies evoked by the breath for the furtherance of its objectives and for world service.

Therefore, we will do no more than see that our breathing is quiet and regular, and will then withdraw our thoughts from the body altogether and begin the work of concentration.

The next step in the practice of meditation is the use of the imagination; we picture to ourselves the threefold lower man, aligned or in direct communication with the soul. There are many ways in which this can be done. We call it work in visualization. It would seem that visualization, imagination and will are three very potent factors in all creative processes. They are the subjective causes for many of our objective effects. At the beginning, visualization is mostly a matter of experimental faith. We know that through the reasoning process, we have arrived at an understanding that, within and beyond all manifested objects, there lies an Ideal Object or Ideal Pattern, which is seeking to become manifest upon the physical plane. The practice of visualization, imagination and the use of the will are activities that are calculated to hasten the manifestation of this Ideal.

When we visualize, we use our highest conception of what that Ideal might be, clothed in some sort of material, usually mental, because we are not yet in a position to be able to conceive of higher forms or types of substance with which to envelop our Images. When we make a mental picture, the mental substance of our mind sets up a certain rate of vibration, which attracts to itself a corresponding grade of mental substance, in which the mind is immersed. It is the will which holds this image steady and which gives it life. This process goes on, whether we are, as yet, able to see it with the mental eye or not. It does not matter that we are not able to see it, as the creative work is going on just the same. Perhaps at some time we shall be able to follow and consciously perform that whole process.

In connection with this work, at the stage of the

beginner, some people picture the three bodies (the three aspects of the form nature) as being linked with a radiant body of light, or they visualize three centres of vibrating energy receiving stimulation from a higher and more powerful centre; others imagine the soul as a triangle of force to which is linked the triangle of the lower nature—linked by the "silver cord" mentioned in the Christian Bible, the sutratma or thread soul of the Eastern Scriptures, the "life-line" of other schools of thought. Still others prefer to preserve the thought of a unified personality, linked to and hiding within itself the indwelling Divinity, Christ in us, the hope of glory. It is relatively immaterial what imagery we choose, provided that we start with the basic idea of the Self seeking to contact and use the Not-self, its instrument in the worlds of human expression, and vice versa, with the thought of that Not-self being impelled to turn itself towards its source of being. Thus, through the use of the imagination and visualization, the desire body, the emotional nature, is brought into line with the soul. When this has been done we can continue with our meditation work. The physical body and the desire nature, in their turn, sink below the level of consciousness, we become centred in the mind and seek to bend it to our will.

It is just here that we find our problem confronting us. The mind refuses to mould itself into the thoughts which we choose to think, and rushes all over the world in its usual quest for material. We think of what we are going to do that day, instead of thinking upon our "seed-thought," we remember some one we must manage to see, or some line of action which calls for attention; we begin to think of some one we love, and immediately we drop back into the world of the emotions and have all our work to do over again. So we re-collect our thoughts and start afresh with much success for half a minute, and then we remember some appointment we have made, or some piece of business which some one is doing for us, and again we are back in the world of mental reactions, and our chosen line of thought is forgotten. Again we re-collect our scattered ideas and recommence our labor of reducing the wayward mind to submission.

Will Levington Comfort, in his 113th Letter, sums this up for us as follows:

"Our shattered attention—we do not dream how shattered until we begin to concentrate, until from the practice of concentration, a new fairness and fixity dawns, in the midst of the seething ineffectiveness of personal life. In our earlier attempts at meditation, we jumped over such commonplace instructions as choosing the subject, and holding the mind closely and faithfully to it; we rushed past all that, passion for ecstasy, for initiation, for means by which we could shine and lord it over others. We were permitted to pasture up in the boggy meadows of emotion, calling them the bright fields of spirit; we were permitted to think we think . . . until in the pinch of lack, or the droop of importance, the breath-taking uncertainties and instabilities of our ground-work were shown up. Convinced at last, we became very eager to begin all over again at the bottom, and the word Stability looms.''[4]

He goes on in the same letter to tell us that

''Our concentrations are breathless at first from the very effort we put into them. This rigidity fends off the results we seek for a time, but with practice we become skilful at length in holding a mental one-pointedness with a kind of effortless content which may safely be empowered.''[5]

How is this condition of empowering reached? By following a form or outline in our meditation work which automatically sets a ring-pass-not around the mind, and which says to the mind, ''thus far shalt thou go, and no farther.'' We deliberately and with intelligent intent set the limits of our mental activity in such a form that we are forced to recognize when we stray beyond those limits. We know then that we must retire again within the sheltering wall we have defined for ourselves. This following of a form in meditation is necessary usually for several years, unless one has had previous practice, and usually even those who have arrived at the stage of contemplation test themselves out quite often by the use of a form in order to make sure that they are not dropping back into a negative emotional quiescent state.

I have used such forms as the following in working with approximately three thousand students of the meditation technique during the last seven years,

[4] Comfort, Will Levington, *Letters.*
[5] *Ibid.*

and it has proved itself in so many cases that I am including it here.

MEDITATION FORM

To Develop Concentration

Stages

1. The attainment of physical comfort and control.
2. The breathing is noted as rhythmic and regular.
3. Visualization of the threefold lower self (physical, emotional and mental) as
   a. In contact with the soul.
   b. As a channel for soul energy, through the medium of the mind, direct to the brain. From thence the physical mechanism can be controlled.
4. Then a definite act of concentration, calling in the will. This involves an endeavor to keep the mind unmoving upon a certain form of words, so that their meaning is clear in our consciousness, and not the words themselves, or the fact that we are attempting to meditate.
5. Then say, with focussed attention—
   "More radiant than the sun, purer than the snow, subtler than the ether is the Self, The spirit within me. I am that Self. That Self am I."
6. Concentrate now upon the words: "Thou God seest me." The mind is not permitted to falter in its concentration on their significance, meaning, and implications.
7. Then, with deliberation bring the concentration work to a close, and say—again with the mind re-focussed on the underlying ideas—the following concluding statement:
   "There is a peace that passeth understanding; it abides in the hearts of those who live in the Eternal. There is a power that maketh all things new; it lives and moves in those who know the Self as one."

This is definitely a beginner's meditation. It has several focal points in it where a re-collection process and a re-focussing method is employed. There are many other meditation outlines which can bring about the same results, and many more that are for advanced workers. There are meditation outlines which are drawn up to produce certain specific results in particular people, but it is obvious that they cannot be included in such a book as this. A safe and general meditation form is all that is possible. In all of them, however, the primary thing to bear in mind is that the mind must be kept *actively occupied with ideas* and not with the effort to be concentrated. Behind every word spoken, and every stage followed there must be the will to understand and a mental activity of a one-pointed nature.

In the sixth stage where the effort is made to meditate definitely upon a form of words, veiling a truth, there should be nothing automatic in the process. It is quite easy to induce in oneself an hypnotic condition by the rhythmic repetition of certain words. We are told that Tennyson induced in himself a heightened state of consciousness by the repetition of his own name. This is not our object. The trance or automatic condition is dangerous. The safe way is that of an intense mental activity, confined within the field of ideas opened up by any particular "seed-thought" or object in meditation. This activity excludes all extraneous thoughts, except those which the words under consideration arouse. The words taken in this particular form can illustrate this, and the process depicts a sequence of thought as follows:

> Thou God seest me.
>
> This God is the divine in me, the indwelling Christ, the Soul.
>
> For long ages this soul has perceived and observed me.
>
> Now for the first time I am in a position to see God.
>
> Up till now, I have been negative to this divine Reality.
>
> The positive relation is becoming possible.
>
> But—this seems to involve the idea of duality.
>
> But I and God are one.
>
> I am God, and have been all the time.
>
> Therefore I have been seen by my Self.
>
> I am that Self, That Self am I.

This is easily written down, but if the mind is kept actively intent upon the sense and meaning, much hard and focussed thinking will have to be done, and much difficulty will be found to eliminate all thoughts other than those having a bearing upon the subject. Sometimes I have found it helpful to say to the puzzled beginner, who is discouraged by his inability to think when and as he chooses: "Imagine you have to give a lecture upon these words to an audience. Picture yourself as formulating the notes upon which you will later speak. Carry your mind on from stage to stage and you will find that five minutes will have gone by without your attention wavering, so great will have been your interest.''

Verses should be chosen which are positive in their effect. Those that induce a waiting and negative state of mind should be avoided. A certain amount of realization and experience is necessary before such words (so frequently chosen by well-meaning beginners) as ''be still, and know that I am God,'' can be safely carried into the meditation work. The call for too great a quiescence of the untrained personality, and the energy they evoke goes to the stimulation of the psychic nature. Mr. Comfort points this out most beautifully in the same letter.

''I believe that such meditations as 'be still and know I am God,' if strenuously indulged in may prove disastrous. More than one unripe personality has opened within itself receptivity to power which played upon its unfulfillments, arousing secret passions and ambitions beyond his power to cope with. The meditation 'I am God' might therefore, be said to be almost too direct and efficacious until such time as the workman knows exactly what he is about. One cannot play up to the Ego and continue long to act the part before men. The end of that is disease and desperate fatigue and loss of the way while shouting it to others. This is not a matter of getting something to show men. It is a matter of understanding what we are made of as personalities; of sensing the Key to a new potency altogether and of rendering with ardent entirety the whole human nature to the game of reaching and turning that Key. I realize that this paragraph touching the 'I am God' meditation contains a lure as well as a warning. It is quite true that the time must come for all of us when we shall operate from the office of the Ego, instead of from the personality, but a fine integrity of the personality must be established before we can carry the power.''[6]

The sequential method suggested above is a safe way for the neophyte. There are others that will occur to the mind of the intelligent student. Whole worlds of thought are open over which the mind can range at will (note those words) provided they have a bearing upon the seed-thought and have a definite relation to the chosen idea upon which we seek to concentrate. It is obvious that each person will follow the bent of his own mind—artistic, scientific or philosophical—and for them that will be the line of least resistance. We shall all formulate our own concepts in our own way. But the ''Be still'' attitude is not for us. We inhibit other mental activities by an intense interest, not by a mental stunning of ourselves into silence, or by the adoption of a method which induces trance or utter thoughtlessness. We are definitely thinking. Any person who is teaching meditation knows how difficult it is to induce the mystic to renounce his quiescent condition (which is the result of an endeavor to make the emotional nature one-pointed) and force him to begin to use his mind. How often one hears the complaint: ''I do not like this technique; it is too intellectual and mental and not a bit spiritual.'' What they really mean is something like this: ''I am too lazy to use my mind; I suffer from mental inertia; I much prefer emotional rhapsodies, and the imposition of a peaceful state upon my emotional nature. I feel

[6] Comfort, Will Levington, *Letters.*

better. This way involves too much hard work.''
Why should spirituality be confounded with emotions? Why should not knowledge be just as divine
as feeling? Of course, this way does involve hard
work, particularly at first. But it can be done, if
the initial laziness can be overcome, and those who
have achieved know of its supreme value.

In concluding this attempt to indicate the initial
work that the aspirant to this way has to undertake,
it should be noted that the key to success lies in constant and unremitting practice. Often, in our work
with students all over the world, we find the brilliant
mind coming out second, because it lacks persevering effort, and the more ordinary mind suddenly
breaking through into the realm of ascertained
knowledge and leaving its more brilliant brother
behind, because it possesses the capacity to keep on
going on. Sporadic efforts get the aspirant nowhere;
in fact they are definitely harmful, inasmuch as they
breed a constant sense of failure. A little consistent
and faithful work done every day, over a long period
of time, will bring results infinitely greater than
enthusiastic but spasmodic efforts. A few minutes
of concentration or meditation work done with
regularity, will carry the aspirant much farther than
hours of effort given three or four times a month.
It has been truly said that ''meditation to be effective in producing results must not be merely a
sporadic effort in which we engage when we feel inclined, but it is a steady unremitting pressure of the
will.''

Another point to be remembered is that the last person to appreciate the results of his work is the student himself. The goal he has set himself is so wonderful, that he is more apt to be discouraged than satisfied. The only wise thing to do is to put all thought of eventual results and their phenomenal effects entirely out of the mind definitely, once and for all, and simply follow the ancient rules. This must be done without a constant plucking of oneself up by the roots to see how one is growing. Those around us will know surely and truly what progress we are making by our increased efficiency, self-control, stability and helpfulness. We have found it wise to gauge the growth of a student in the meditation work by the extension of his field of service and by the things his friends say of him, rather than by his own reports about himself. Our work is to go steadily forward, doing the demanded task "without attachment" as the Hindu aspirant calls it.

If success is to be achieved, there must be a genuine and persistent desire, a clear picture of the value of the results, a realization that the goal can be achieved and definite knowledge of the technique of the method. This, with the unremitting pressure of the will is all that is needed, and this is possible for every reader of this book.

CHAPTER TEN

THE NEED FOR CARE IN MEDITATION

"A clean life, an open mind, a pure heart, an eager intellect, an unveiled spiritual perception, a brotherliness for one's co-disciple, a readiness to give and receive advice and instruction, . . . a willing obedience to the behests of Truth, . . . a courageous endurance of personal injustice, a brave declaration of principles, a valiant defence of those who are unjustly attacked, and a constant eye to the ideal of human progression and perfection which the secret science depicts; these are the golden stairs up the steps of which the learner may climb to the Temple of Divine Wisdom."

H. P. BLAVATSKY

The Need for Care in Meditation

THE meditation work outline in the previous chapter constitutes a good concentration exercise for the beginner and will eventually lead him—if he possesses persistence—to the genuine practice of meditation. A concentration that lasts one minute is difficult to achieve but is a real step upon the way to meditation, which is the act of prolonged concentration. The outline will help to produce the condition of active attention. Many such outlines are available, and can be drawn up, by those who know the rules and who are good psychologists, to suit the needs of differing types of people. A few such outlines will be found at the close of the book, but it is obvious that in a book of this description the more advanced practices and the more intensive work have no place. They can be wisely carried forward only when the earlier stages have been mastered.

It should be noted that any thought process, followed with undeviating attention, which leads "inward" from the outer form to the energy or life aspect of that form and which enables the thinker to be identified with it, will serve a purpose similar to a technical outline. Any noun, for instance, when properly understood as the name of a thing and, therefore, of a form, will serve as a seed thought in meditation. The form will be studied as to its quality and purpose, and all can in time be traced back to an idea, and all true ideas emanate from the realm of the soul. If the right attitude, therefore is assumed and the processes outlined in Chapter Five are followed, the thinker will find himself led out of the phenomenal world into the world of Divine Realities. As practice in concentration is gained, the consideration of the outer form, and of its quality and aspect can be omitted, and the act of concentration, having become (through persistence and practice) automatic and instantaneous, the student can start with the *purpose* aspect, or with the underlying idea which brought the outer form into being. This entire concept has been expressed for us by Plutarch in these words:

"An idea is a Being incorporeal, which has no subsistence of itself, but gives figure and form unto shapeless matter and becomes the cause of the manifestation." (**De** *Placit. Philos.*)

These are significant words and hold much information for the student of this ancient technique of meditation.

The goal of meditation, from the angle of the mind, might therefore, be stated to be the attainment of the world of ideas; from the angle of the soul, it is the identification of the individual soul with the world originator of all ideas. Through mind control, we become aware of the ideas which lie back of our world evolution, and the manifestation (through matter) of the form that they take. Through meditation, we contact a part of the Plan; we see the blue prints of the Great Architect of the Universe, and are given opportunity to participate in their emergence into objective being through our contact with, and right interpretation of, the ideas we succeed in contacting in meditation.

It will, therefore, be apparent how necessary it is that the aspirant should be possessed of a well trained and well-stocked mind, if he is to interpret with accuracy that which he sees; it is evident that he should be able to formulate with clarity the thoughts with which he seeks to clothe the nebulous ideas, and in turn, through this clear thinking, impress the waiting brain. It may be true that "God" works out, in many cases, His plans through the agency of human beings, but He needs intelligent agents; He needs men and women who are not more stupid than those chosen by the leaders of the race to participate in their endeavors. Just to love God is not entirely sufficient. It is a step in the right direction, but devotion, unbalanced by good sense and brains, leads to much stupid action and much unconsidered effort. God looks for those who have trained and highly developed minds, and fine brains (to act as sensitive recorders of the higher impressions), so that the work may be carried forward rightly. Perhaps it might be said that the saints and mystics have revealed to us the nature of the Divine Life, and the quality of the ideas which govern Hiactivities in the world of phenomena, and that the knowers of the world and the intellectuals of the race must, in their turn, reveal to the world the synthetic Plan and the Divine Purpose. Thus shall we find the thread of gold which will guide us out of the maze of our present chaotic world condition into the light of truth and of understanding.

It should be remembered that we live in a world of energies and of forces. The power of public opinion (emotional as it usually is, and frequently set in motion by some basic ideas, formulated by thinkers, good, bad and indifferent) is well known, and is a form of energy, producing big results. The devastating effect of uncontrolled emotion, for instance, is equally well known, and is again a demonstration of force. The expression, so constantly used, "the forces of nature," shows us that since man began to think at all he has known that all is energy. The scientists tell us that everything is a manifestation of energy. There is nothing but energy, pouring through us, and working in us, and in it we are immersed. All forms are built of atoms, we are told, and atoms are units of energy. Man, therefore, is himself energy, formed of energy units, living in a world similarly constituted and working with energy all the time.

The fundamental law governing all meditation work is the ancient one formulated by the seers in India centuries ago, that "energy follows thought." From the realm of ideas (or of soul knowledge) energy pours through. The "public opinion" of the soul realm seeps little by little into the dense minds of men, and to it can be traced all the forward movements of the present time, all organization of general welfare and of group betterment; all religious concepts and all outer knowledge of the Causes which produce objectivity. These ideas assume a mental form, first of all, and some mind grasps them and ponders upon them, or passes them on to some group of thinkers, and the work of "thinking through" goes forward. Then the quality of desire begins to enter in, and there is an emotional reaction to the thoughts which the ideas have evoked, and the form is gradually built. Thus the work goes on and the energy of the soul and of the mind and of the desire nature correlate with the energy of matter, and a definite form comes into being. Every form, whether it be the form of a sewing machine, of a social order or of a solar system, can be posited as the materialization of the thought of some thinker, or of some group of thinkers. It is a form of creative work, and the same laws of emergence into being have governed the entire process, and all the work has been concentrated with energy of some type or another. The student of meditation must, therefore, remember that he is always working with energies, and that these varying energies will have a definite effect upon the energies of which he himself is composed (if such an expression is permissible).

It will be apparent, therefore, that the man who is learning to meditate must endeavor to do two things:

First: He must learn to "bring through" into his

mind and then interpret correctly what he has seen and contacted, and later transmit it correctly and accurately to the attentive and impressionable brain. Thus the man, in physical waking consciousness becomes aware of the things of the Kingdom of God.

Second: He must learn the nature of the energies he is contacting, and train himself to utilize them correctly. A practical illustration of this can be given here, and one universally recognized. We are swept by anger or irritation. Instinctively we begin to shout. Why? Emotional energy has us in its grip. By learning to control the energy of the spoken word we begin to master that particular type of emotional energy.

In these two ideas of right interpretation and right transmission, and of right use of energy, the whole story of the meditation work is summed up. It becomes apparent also what is the problem confronting the student, and why all wise teachers of the technique of meditation urge upon their pupils the need of care and slow procedure.

It is essential that we realize that meditation can be very dangerous work and may land a man in serious difficulty. It can be destructive and disrupting; it can do more harm than good and lead a man towards catastrophe if he enters upon the Way of the Knower without a proper understanding of what he is doing and where it will lead him. At the same time, it can be, indeed, the "work of salvation" and lead a man out of all his difficulties; it can be constructive and liberating, and guide the man by right and sane methods along the way that leads from darkness to light, from death to immortality, and from the unreal to the Real.

It might be of value here if we considered these two points a little more closely.

We have seen that the deep need of the aspirant is to see that he succeeds in bringing through into his physical brain-consciousness, with accuracy, the phenomena of the spiritual world which he may succeed in contacting. The probability is, however, that it will be a long time before he can penetrate into that world at all. Therefore, he has to learn to discriminate between the fields of awareness which may open up before him as he becomes more sensitive, and know the nature of what he is seeing and hearing. Let us look for a moment at some of the phenomena of the lower mind which students are so constantly misinterpreting.

They record, for instance, a rapturous encounter with the Christ or with some Great Soul, who appeared to them when meditating, smiled at them, and told them to "be of good cheer. You are making good progress. You are a chosen worker and to you truth shall be revealed," or something equally fatuous. They thrill to the event; they record it in their diary and they write joyously to me that the occurrence is a most momentous happening in their lives. It may be, if they handle it right, and learn its lesson. What has really happened? Has the student really seen the Christ? Here we remember the truism that "thoughts are things" and that all

thoughts take form. Two things have produced the
occurrence, if it has really happened and is not the
result of a vivid and overstimulated imagination.
The power of the creative imagination is only just
beginning to be sensed, and it is quite possible to see
just what we desire to see, even if it is not there at
all. The desire of the aspirant to make progress, and
his strenuous effort, has forced him to become awake
or aware upon the psychic plane, the plane of vain
imaginings, of desire and its illusory fulfillments.
In that realm, he contacts a thought-form of the
Christ or of some great and revered Teacher. The
world of illusion is full of these thought-forms, con-
structed by the loving thoughts of men down the
ages, and the man, working through his own psychic
nature (the line of least resistance for the majority)
comes in touch with such a thought-form, mistakes
it for the real, and imagines it saying to him all the
things he wants said. He wants encouragement; he
seeks, like so many, the justification of phenomena
for his endeavor; he quiets the brain and gently
slips into a psychic and negative condition. Whilst
in that condition, his imagination begins to function,
and he sees what he wants to see, and he hears the
magnificent words of recognition for which he
hankers. It does not occur to him that the Guides of
the race are too busy with group activities and with
the training of the advanced thinkers and leaders of
humanity, through whom They *can* work, to spend
any time with the children of the race. The latter
may be left, with complete success, to the tuition of

less highly evolved beings. Nor does it occur to them that, should they be so advanced and so highly evolved as to have won the privilege of making such a contact, the Master would not waste His time and theirs by patting them on the back and pronouncing high sounding but inane platitudes. He would improve the brief moment by pointing out some weakness to be eliminated, or some constructive work to be undertaken.

Again, some "force"—a word frequently used—or some entity comes to the student, as he meditates, and outlines to him some great work that he has been chosen to do; some world message that he has to give and to which the entire world is to listen, or some great invention he is to present some day to a waiting world if he continues to be good. Gladly he grasps the mantle of the prophet, and with unshaken belief in his capacity, his ability to influence thousands, even if he is relatively impotent to influence those around him at present, he prepares to carry out his divine mission. In one year, three "World Teachers," who have been studying meditation in some school or other, made application to the group with whom I am associated. This they did, not because they wanted to carry their meditation forward, but because they felt we would be happy to have them "feed" into the group some of the many hundreds they were to be instrumental in saving. I had to decline the honor, and they disappeared, and nothing has since been heard of them. The world still awaits them. Of their sincerity there is absolutely no doubt. They believed what they said. Neither is there any doubt of their being hallucinated. All of us are in danger of being deluded in just this way, when we start to meditate, if the discriminating mind is not on the watch, or if we have a secret longing for spiritual prominence, or suffer from an inferiority complex which must be offset. Another cause for the delusion lies in the fact that these people have perhaps made a real contact with the soul. They have had a flash of its omniscience and are swept off their feet by the very wonder of the contacted vision and knowledge. But they overestimate their capacity; the instrument of the soul is totally unable to measure up to requirements; there are aspects of their life upon which the light may not shine; there are secret faults which they know but cannot break; there is the desire for fame and power; there is ambition. They are not yet the soul in functioning activity. They have simply had a vision of a possibility. Hence they crash through their failure to see the personality as it is.

Yet, in spite of the truth of the above, let us always remember that it *is* the privilege of the true knower to work in the closest co-operation with the Guides of the race, but that the method of co-operation is not the one which deceived the aspirant. Only when we have begun consciously to function as souls, and only when we are busy with self-forgetting service —a service that is self-initiated, and carried forward because the soul is group conscious, and it is in the nature of the soul to serve—will we make such a contact. The Christ is the Son of God in full functioning activity, the "Eldest in a great family of brothers." He has a consciousness which is universal in its scope, and through Him the love of God pours, and the purposes of God are working to fruition. He is the Master of all the Masters, and the Teacher alike of Angels and of men. When He and those associated with Him find an aspirant who is engrossed with the work to be done in self-discipline, who is faithful and conscientious in his endeavor, they look to see if the light within him has reached the point of "the shining forth." If they find one who is so anxious to serve his fellowmen that he is looking for no phenomenal contacts for himself and is not interested in being patted on the back and having his pride and self-satisfaction fed in this manner, then they may reveal to him the work that he can do in his own sphere of influence to further the Divine Plan. But he will have to begin where he is; he will have to make his demonstration first of all in his home or office; he will have to prove himself in the small things before he can be safely trusted with the big. The ludicrous arrogance of some of the writings which record the psychic contacts of the writers is almost beyond belief. They certainly lack a sense of humor at least.

The point that every student of meditation should always bear in mind is that all knowledge and instructions are conveyed to the mind and brain by a man's own soul; it is the soul that illumines his way. The Teachers and Masters of the race work through souls. This cannot be too often reiterated. Therefore, the prime duty of every aspirant should be the perfect performance of meditation and service and discipline, and not the making of contact with some great Soul. It is less interesting, but preserves him from illusion. If he does this, the higher results will take care of themselves. Should an apparition appear to him, therefore, and should such an entity make platitudinous comments, he will use the same judgment as he would in business or ordinary life with a man who came and said to him, "A great work lies in your hands, you are doing well. We see and know, etc., etc." He would probably laugh and continue with the activity or duty of the moment.

Another effect of meditation, and a very prevalent one at this time, is the flood of so-called inspirational writings which are coming out, with high claims made for them, everywhere. Men and women are busily writing automatically, inspirationally, and prophetically, and giving to the public the result of their labors. These writings are distinguished by certain uniform features and can be explained in several ways. They emanate from many different interior sources. They are curiously alike; they indicate a lovely aspirational spirit; they say no new thing, but repeat what has often been said before; they are full of statements and phrases which link them up with the writings of the mystics or with the Christian teaching; they may contain prophecies as to future events (usually dire and dreadful, and seldom, if ever, of a happy nature); they carry much comfort to the writer and make him feel he is a great and wonderful soul; and, fortunately, they are generally innocuous. Their name is legion, and they become exceedingly tiresome after one has toiled through a few of the manuscripts. Some few are definitely destructive. They foretell great and immediate cataclysms, and breed fear in the world. Even suppose these predictions are true, one is tempted to ask whether anything is gained by frightening the public and whether it is not more constructive to build the realization of their immortal destiny into people than to tell them they are going down in a tidal wave, or will be submerged in the catastrophe which is going to wipe their particular city off the map. What are these writings—good and innocuous, or harmful and destructive and subversive of public order? They fall roughly into two classes. First, there are the writings of those sensitive souls who can tune in—again on psychic levels—with the mass of aspirations, longings and ideas of the mystics of all times, or, equally, they can tune in on the fears of the ages, the racial and hereditary fears, or the fears engendered by world conditions prevailing at this time. These they record and write down and hand around to their friends. Under this category come the writings of those who are sensitive in a more mental manner, and can tune in telepathically with the mental world; they are responsive to the mind of some powerful thinker, or to the massed concepts of the religious world; they register, on mental levels, the fear and hatred and separativeness of the masses. Whether the material they record is good or bad, whether it is happy, which it seldom is, or unhappy in nature, and whether it carries a vibration of fear and foreboding, it is all psychic stuff, and it in no way indicates the revealing quality of the soul. The prophecies in the Books of Daniel and Revelations have been responsible for the building up of a thought-form of fear and of terror which has led to much writing of a psychic nature, and the exclusiveness of organized religion has led many to separate themselves off from the rest of humanity and to regard themselves as the elect of the Lord, with the mark of the Christ on their foreheads and, therefore, to take the position that they are safe and the rest of the world must perish, unless they can be brought to interpret truth and the future in the exclusive terms of the anointed and select.

Secondly, these writings can indicate a process of self unfoldment, and a method whereby the introverted mystic can become the extrovert. The writer may be tapping the wealth of the subconscious knowledge which is his, and which he has accumulated through his reading, thinking and contacts. His mind has recorded and stored up much of which he remains for years totally unaware. Then he begins to meditate and suddenly taps the depths of his own nature and penetrates to the resources of his own subconsciousness and to information which has dropped below the threshold of his ordinary consciousness. He begins to write assiduously. Why he should regard these thoughts as emanating from the

Christ, or from some great Teacher is a puzzle. It probably feeds his pride—again quite unconsciously —to feel he is a channel through which the Christ can communicate. I am not referring here to the mass of automatic writings which are so popular now. I am supposing that the student of meditation refuses to have anything to do with this kind of dangerous work. No true aspirant, in his efforts to be master of himself, will hand over the reins of government and submit to the control of any entity, incarnate or discarnate; neither will he render up his hand blindly for any force to use. The dangers of this kind of work are becoming too well known and have landed so many people in the psychopathic wards, or necessitated their being freed from obsessions or from "idées fixes", that there is no need for me to enlarge upon it.

How, it might be pertinently asked, can one distinguish between the truly inspired writings of the true knower, and this mass of literature which is flooding the minds of the public at this time? First, I should say that the true inspirational writing will be entirely without self-reference; it will sound a note of love and will be free from hatreds and racial barriers; it will convey definite knowledge and carry a note of authority by its appeal to the intuition; it will respond to the law of correspondences, and fit into the world picture; above all, it will carry the impress of Divine Wisdom and lead the race on a little further. As to its mechanics; the writers of such a type of teaching will have a real understanding of the methods they employ. They will have mastered the technique of the process; they will be able to guard themselves from illusion, and from the intrusion of personalities, and will have a working knowledge of the apparatus with which they are working. If they are receiving teachings from discarnate entities, and from great Masters, they will know how to receive it, and will then know all about the agent transmitting the teaching.

True servers of the race and those who have contacted the world of the soul, through meditation, have no time for platitudes; these can safely be left to the parrots of the world; they are too busy serving constructively to care to pick up mantles which are only a veil to pride; they are not interested in the good opinion of any person, incarnate or discarnate, and care only for the approval of their own soul, and are vitally interested in the pioneering work of the world. They will do nothing to feed hatred and separativeness or to foster fear. There are numbers of people in the world only too ready to do that. They will fan the flame of love wherever they go; they will teach brotherhood in its true inclusiveness, and not a system which will teach brotherhood to a few and leave the rest outside. They will recognize all men as sons of God and will not set themselves upon a pedestal of righteousness and knowledge from whence they proclaim the truth as they see it and consign those to destruction who do not see as they do, or do not act as they feel they should, placing them outside the pale; they will not regard one race as better than another, though they may recognize the evolutionary plan and the work that each race has to do. They will, in short, occupy themselves by building up the characters of men, and not waste their time in tearing down personalities, and dealing with effects and with results. They work in the world of causes, and enunciate principles. The world is full of those who tear down, and who feed the present hatreds, and who widen the divisions between races and groups, between rich and poor. Let the true student of meditation remember that when he makes a contact with his soul, and becomes at-one with Reality, he is entering into a state of group awareness, which breaks down all barriers, and leaves none of the sons of God outside its field of knowledge.

It is possible to mention other forms of illusion, for the first world the aspirant contacts seems usually to be the psychic world, and that is the world of illusion. This world of illusion has its uses, and entering it is a most valuable experience, provided that the rule of love and of non-self-reference is carried there, and that all contacts made are subjected to the discriminating mind and ordinary commonsense. So many aspirants lack a sense of humor, and take themselves far too seriously. They seem to leave behind them their good sense, when they enter a new field of phenomena. It is useful to record what is seen and heard and then to forget about it until such time as we have begun to function in the kingdom of the soul; then we will be no longer interested in its recollection. We must also avoid personalities and pride, for they have no place in the life of the soul, which is governed by principles and love to all beings. If these things are developed, there is no danger of any student of meditation being side-tracked, or delayed; he will inevitably enter some day into that world of which it is said "eye hath not seen or ear heard, the things which God hath revealed to them that love him", the time being dependent upon his persistence and patience.

The second type of difficulty which we should consider is the one that can be interpreted in terms of energy.

Students frequently complain of over-stimulation and of such an increased energy that they find themselves unable to cope with it. They tell us that, when attempting to meditate, they have an inclination to weep, or to be unduly restless; they have periods of intense activity wherein they find themselves running hither and thither serving, talking, writing and working so that they end by undergoing a violent reaction, sometimes to the point of nervous collapse. Others complain of pains in the head, of headaches immediately after meditating, or of an uncomfortable vibration in the forehead, or the throat. They also find themselves unable to sleep as well as heretofore. They are, in fact, over-stimulated. The nervous system is being affected through the medium of the fine and subtle "nadis" which underly the nerves and to which we earlier referred. These troubles are the troubles of the neophyte in the science of meditation and must be dealt with carefully. Rightly handled, they will soon disappear, but if they are ignored they may lead to serious trouble. The earnest and interested aspirant, at this stage, is himself a difficulty, for he is so anxious to master the technique of meditation, that he ignores the rules given him and drives himself, in spite of all the teacher may say or the warnings he may receive. Instead of adhering to the fifteen minute formula which is given him, he endeavors to force the pace and do thirty minutes; instead of following his outline, which is so arranged that it takes about fifteen minutes to complete, he tries to hold the concentration as long as possible, and at the height of his effort, forgetting that he is learning to *concentrate*, and not to meditate, at this stage of his training. So he suffers, and has a nervous breakdown, or a spell of insomnia, and his teacher gets the blame and the science is regarded as dangerous. Yet all the time, he himself is the one in fault.

When some of these primary troubles occur, the meditation work should be temporarily stopped, or slowed down. If the condition is not sufficiently serious to warrant the complete cessation of the work, a close observation should be made of where (in the human body) the inflowing energy seems to go. Energy is tapped in meditation, and it will find its way to some part or other of the mechanism.

In *mental* types, or in the case of those who have already some facility in "centering the consciousness" in the head, it is the brain cells which become

over-stimulated, leading to headaches, to sleepless-
ness, to a sense of fulness, or to a disturbing vibration between the eyes or at the very top of the head.
Sometimes there is a sense of blinding light, like
a sudden flash of lightning or of electricity, registered when the eyes are closed, and in the dark
equally as in the light.

When this is the case, the meditation period should
be reduced from fifteen minutes to five, or meditation should be practised on alternate days, until such
time as the brain cells have adjusted themselves to
the new rhythm and the increased stimulation. There
is no need for anxiety, if wise judgment is used,
and obedience to the advice of the teacher is present,
but should the student at this time begin to push
his meditation, or to increase the time period, he
may lay up for himself a good deal of trouble. Again
common-sense comes into play, and with the reduc-
tion of the time, and with the practice of a little
meditation every day, it should soon be possible to
bring the work back again to normal. We have had
students who have suffered this way, but who, by
obedience to suggested rules, and the use of common-
sense, are now doing their thirty minutes' or an
hour's meditation daily.

In *emotional* types, the trouble is first sensed in
the region of the solar plexus. The student finds
himself prone to irritation and to anxiety and
worry; also, particularly in the case of women, there
may be found a disposition to cry easily. Sometimes
there is a tendency to nausea, for there is a close

relation between the emotional nature and the stomach, as is evidenced by frequency of vomiting in moments of shock, or fright, or intense emotion. The same rules apply as in the first set of cases:—common-sense and a careful and slower use of the meditation process.

Another result of over-stimulation might be mentioned. People find themselves becoming over-sensitive. The senses work overtime and all their reactions are more acute. They "take on" the conditions, physical or psychic, of those with whom they live; they find themselves "wide open" to the thoughts and moods of other people. The cure for this is not to lessen the meditation periods—these should be continued as per schedule,—but to become more mentally interested in life, in the thought world, in some subject which will tend to develop the mental capacity and so bring about the ability to live in the head and not in the emotional region. Focussed attention to life and its problems, and some potent mental occupation will effect a cure. It is for this reason that wise teachers of meditation parallel the meditation work with some course of reading and study, so as to preserve the balance of their students. A rounded out development is needed always, and a trained mind should accompany growth in the spiritual life.

There is a third category of undesirable results which should not be omitted. Many students of meditation complain that their sex life has been tremendously stimulated and is giving them much trouble.

We have come across such cases. On investigation, it will usually be found that these students are people whose animal nature is very strong, who have led an active and ill-regulated sex life, or whose thoughts are much engrossed with sex, even if the physical life is controlled. A strong mental complex as to sex is often discovered, and people who would regard it as wrong to lead an abnormal sex life, or to practice perversions, are mentally occupying themselves with sex or are discussing it all the time and letting it play an undue part in their thought life.

Some most worthy people have also a settled conviction that celibacy must always accompany the life of the spirit. May it not be possible that the true celibacy to which the ancient rules are intended to refer concerns the attitude of the soul, or spiritual man, to the world, the flesh and the devil, as our Christian Scriptures put it? May not the true celibacy have reference to our abstaining from all appearance of evil? This may in one man involve his abstaining from all sex relations in order to demonstrate to himself his control over the animal nature; in other cases, it may, for instance, involve refraining from all gossip and idle speech. There is nothing sinful in marriage and it is probably the way out for many who would otherwise lead an unduly active mental life where sex is concerned. It is needless, surely, to add here that the true student of meditation should not tolerate in his life promiscuous or illegitimate sexual relations. The aspirant to the life of the spirit conforms not only to the laws of the spiritual kingdom but to the legalized customs of his age and time. He, therefore, regularizes his physical every day life so that the man in the street recognizes the morality, the uprightness and the correctness of his presentation to the world. A home that is based upon a true and happy relation between a man and a woman, upon mutual trust, co-operation and understanding, and in which the principles of spiritual living are emphasized, is one of the finest aids that can be given to the world at this time. A relation that is based on physical attraction and the gratification of the sex nature, and which has, as its primary objective, the prostitution of the physical nature to animal desire, is evil and wrong. If the goal of our effort is to demonstrate God immanent in form, then no level of consciousness is more intrinsically divine than another, and divinity can be expressed in all human relations. If a married man or woman cannot attain illumination and achieve the goal, then there is something wrong and divinity cannot express itself on one plane, at least, of expression; to put in terms that may sound blasphemous but which will enable us to grasp the futility of these reasonings: God is defeated in one part of His Kingdom.

This point has been enlarged upon because so many people, and particularly men, find that the animal nature requires attention when they begin to meditate. They discover within themselves uncontrolled desires, plus physiological effects which cause them acute trouble and discouragement. A person may have a high aspiration and a strong urge towards spiritual living and yet have aspects of his nature still uncontrolled. The energy that pours in during meditation pours down through the mechanism and stimulates the entire sex apparatus. The weak point is always discovered and stimulated. The cure for this situation can be summed up in the words:—control of the thought life and transmutation. An intense mental preoccupation and interest should be cultivated in other directions than the line of least resistance—sex. There should be an endeavor at all times to keep the energy contacted in the head and to permit it to work out through creative activity of some kind. The eastern teaching tells us that energy, usually directed to the functioning of the sex life, has to be raised and carried to the head and throat, particularly the latter, as it is, we are told, the centre of creative work. To put it in western terms, this means that we learn to transmute the energy utilized in the procreative process or in sex thoughts and use it in the work of creative writing, in artistic endeavor, or in some expression of group activity. The tendency in modern times to find the one-pointed thinker and purely mental type evading marriage and as he frequently does leading a purely celibate life, may be a demonstration of the truth of the eastern position. It is causing a good deal of concern among those who study our falling birth rate. Transmutation is not surely the death of an activity or a cessation of functioning on any level of consciousness for the sake of a higher. It is the right utilization of the various aspects of energy wherever the Self feels they should be used for the furthering of the ends of evolution, and the helping of the Plan. The mind, illumined by the soul, should be the controlling factor, and when we think straight, live straight, and raise all thoughts and energies into the "Heavenly places" we shall solve our problems through the development of a spiritual normality which is greatly needed at this time, particularly among aspirants and esoteric students.

It might be well also, before this chapter comes to a close, to refer to the dangers to which many are liable if they respond to the appeal of teachers for pupils to "sit for development." They are then taught to meditate upon some centre of energy, usually the solar plexus, sometimes the heart, curiously enough never the head. Meditating upon a centre is based upon the law that energy follows thought, and leads to the direct stimulation of that centre and the resultant demonstration of the particular characteristics for which these focal points—scattered throughout the human body—are responsible. As the majority of people function primarily through the collected energies that lie below the diaphragm (the sex energies and the emotional energies) their stimulation is most dangerous. In view of this, why take risks? Why not be warned by the experience of others? Why not learn to function as the spiritual man from that point, so quaintly described by the Oriental writers, as "the throne between the eyebrows," and from that high place control all aspects of the lower nature, and guide the daily life in the ways of God.

Conclusion

"The spirit within is the long-lost Word,
  Besought by the world of the soul in pain
  Through a world of words which are void and vain.
  O never while shadow and light are blended
  Shall the world's Word-Quest or its woe be ended,
  And never the world of its wounds made whole
  Till the Word made flesh be the Word made soul!"

ARTHUR EDWARD WAITE

Conclusion

WHAT is to be the result of all our effort? Personal satisfaction or a joyous heaven of endless rest and beatitude? God forbid! The search in the world goes on; the cry of humanity rises from the depths and mounts to the very throne of God Himself. From the heart of the Temple of God, to which we may have fought and wrestled our way, we turn back and work on earth. We rest not in our endeavor till the last of the world's seekers has found his way home.

What is going to save this world from its present agony, economic distress, and chaos? What is going to usher in the New Age of brotherhood and group living? Who, or what, will save the world? May it not be the emergence into active being of a group of practical mystics, who, banded together in the sense of a divine unity, work in practical ways on earth? They will not retire into monasteries or to the silent places of the world, no matter how alluring that may appear, but they will participate in the normal life of the planet. They will be the business executives in our great cities; they will carry forward our political programs; they will lead the young along the paths of right education; they will control our economic, social and national destinies. They will do all this from the centre of their being and from the standpoint of the soul; they will know the secret of illumination; they will know how to submit all problems to the omniscience of the soul; they will know the secret of the life that makes all men brothers.

They will recognize all those they meet as Sons of God, but they will know also the signs of the illumined man and with him they will seek to work for the good of the whole. Telepathically they will find each other, and work, therefore, in the closest co-operation.

This group is already in existence and the members of it are in the closest touch with one another. They are to be found in every country in the world, yet daily they meet in the kingdom of the soul. They speak the same language; they have the same ideals; they know no barriers or divisions; they have no hatreds or class distinction; they set up no racial barriers; they see things as they are. They are not wild idealists, but they concentrate on the next step that humanity must take, and not upon the final stages of their own development. They work with worldly wisdom as well as spiritual insight. Above all, they work together and come into touch with one another through the power of a unified realization.

This integrating group of mystics and knowers is the hope of the world and constitutes the World Savior. They are above and beyond all creeds and theologies; they work in all fields of human achievement—the scientific field, the political, the religious, the educational and the philosophical. They are not interested in terminologies, nor do they waste time seeking to impose on others their pet theories, their peculiar terms, or their particular approach to truth. They recognize the truth underlying all presentations and are only interested in the principles of brotherhood, in the emphasizing of essentials and in living the life of the spirit in the world of every day.

They know the meaning of meditation and they are with us now. Ours is the privilege of joining their ranks by submitting ourselves to the technique of meditation, to the discipline of right daily living and to the influence of the pure motive of SERVICE.

Training for new age
discipleship is provided
by the *Arcane School*.
The principles of the
Ageless Wisdom are
presented through esoteric
meditation, study and
service as a *way of life*.

*Write to the publishers
for information.*

INDEX

A

Abstraction —
 in meditation, process, stages,
  213-214
 into head, process, result, 214
 right, definition, 213
Action, five factors involved, 110
All, union with, 195
Aspiration —
 definition, 93
 stage, three parts, results, 97-98
At-one-ment —
 between higher and lower selves,
  72-73
 of soul and personality,
  attainment, 52
Awareness, human states, 34

B

Bhagavad Gita,
 quotations, 73, 78, 100, 110
Blavatsky, H. P., quotations, 138, 235
Brain —
 and soul, intermediary, 87
 cells, over-stimulation,
  correction, 255-256
 centering oneself in, 108, 214
 control by mind, 205
 coordination with mind, 126
 coordination with mind and soul,
  180-181, 205
 functions, 103, 105, 110-111, 123
 illumination, 247
 in meditation process, 211-215
 points of contact, 163-164, 169,
  170-172
 reception of impressions from
  soul, 104
Breathing exercises in meditation,
 220-223
Browning, Robert, quotation, 82-83
Buddhism —
 Chinese, method, 186-188, 194
 Tibetan, method, 185-186, 194

C

Celibacy, true, 258-259
Christ —
 indwelling, meaning, 97
 Son of God, 247
Christianity, method, 193-194
Clairvoyance, nature of, 84
Concentration —
 cultivation, means, 106-107
 definition, 99, 104-105, 106
 development, form, 206, 207,
  228-229
 exercise, results, 108
 stage, 99-108
Conscience, voice, 97
Consciousness, focussing in head,
 212-213, 214, 215
Contemplation —
 act, ascension, 86
 agency, 137-138
 definitions, 99, 139-140, 141
 description, 137-138
 effects, 165
 stage, 132-144
Cosmic Fire, quotation, 113-116
Culture, attainments, 32-33, 35-36

D

Dangers in meditation practices,
 109, 135, 229, 242, 251, 261
Deity, revelation, 55
Desire, transcending, 109
Detachment —
 definition, 97-98
 inducement, 97
Discrimination in meditation,
 need for, 243-262

E

East —
 comparison with West, 5, 677,
  119-120, 123, 147
 education, 42, 44
 system, defects, 42

269